The Kraken Quest: Exploring the Mythical Giants of the Sea

Edward Turner

Published by Oliver Lancaster, 2023.

While every precaution has been taken in the preparation of this book, the publisher assumes no responsibility for errors or omissions, or for damages resulting from the use of the information contained herein.

THE KRAKEN QUEST: EXPLORING THE MYTHICAL GIANTS OF THE SEA

First edition. August 1, 2023.

Copyright © 2023 Edward Turner.

ISBN: 979-8223004448

Written by Edward Turner.

Also by Edward Turner

Ghosts of Paris: Ten Haunted Places in the City of Love

Appalachian Nightmares: The Top 10 Creepy Creatures of the Mountains

Asia's Top Ten Cryptids: Legends, Sightings, and Theories

Beyond the Shadows: Unlocking the Mystery of Bigfoot

Evil Women in History: Uncovering the Gruesome Crimes of Ten Notorious Female Killers

Ghosts of London: Ten Haunted Places in The City

Ghosts of New York: Ten Haunted Places in The Big Apple

Ghosts of Oregon: The Top 10 Haunted Places You Must Visit

Ghosts of the Stage: Ten Hauntings at the Theatre

Missouri Nightmares: The Top 10 Chilling Legends

Mothman Unleashed: Into the Darkened Skies

North America's Top Ten Cryptids: Legends, Sightings, and Theories

Philly's Phantom Encounters: Exploring the City's Most Haunted Places

Secrets of the Deep: The Mystery of the Loch Ness Monster

Unsolved Mysteries: Delving into the Shadows of Infamous Murders

Unveiling the Shadows: A Journey into Financial Crimes and Scandals

The Kraken Quest: Exploring the Mythical Giants of the Sea

Sign up to my free newsletter to get updates on new releases, FREE teaser chapters to upcoming releases and FREE digital short stories.

Or visit https://tinyurl.com/olanc

I never spam and you can unsubscribe at any time.

EDWARD TURNER

Disclaimer

The information provided in this book is based on historical records, scientific research, and folklore. While every effort has been made to ensure accuracy, the existence of mythical creatures like the Kraken cannot be conclusively proven. The book aims to explore cultural heritage and the wonders of the deep while encouraging curiosity and critical thinking.

The Kraken Quest: Exploring the Mythical Giants of the Sea

EDWARD TURNER

EDWARD TURNER

Chapter 1: Introduction to the Kraken

The Kraken, a legendary sea monster of colossal proportions, has captured the imagination of people across various civilizations throughout history. It is a creature deeply ingrained in folklore, mythology, and maritime traditions. While the specifics of the Kraken's appearance and abilities may vary from one culture to another, its ubiquity in global tales suggests a shared fascination with the vast and mysterious oceans. Let us delve into the historical origins and cultural significance of the Kraken in different civilizations:

In Norse mythology, the Kraken is believed to be a terrifying sea monster that lurks off the coasts of Norway and Greenland. It is described as a gigantic cephalopod with immense tentacles that can reach up to a mile long. The Kraken is mentioned in ancient texts, such as the "Örvar-Odds saga" and the "Konungs skuggsjá" ("King's Mirror"), which describe the creature's role in causing deadly whirlpools and drowning sailors. The Kraken's presence in Norse mythology reflects the ancient seafaring culture's fear and respect for the unpredictable power of the sea.

During the Middle Ages, stories of the Kraken spread throughout Europe. Mariners and explorers, navigating treacherous waters, passed down tales of encountering the creature in their travels. One of the most famous accounts is from the 13th-century Icelandic saga "Krákumál," which speaks of a monstrous beast terrorizing sailors in the Atlantic Ocean. The Kraken's legend grew in parallel with Europe's exploration of distant lands and the vast, uncharted oceans, symbolizing the unknown and untamed dangers that awaited intrepid sailors.

In addition to Norse mythology, Scandinavian folklore also adopted the Kraken as a formidable sea creature. It became an integral part of local storytelling, with tales of brave heroes venturing to confront the Kraken and protect their coastal communities. In these stories, the Kraken represented the struggle of humanity against the overwhelming forces of nature, emphasizing the importance of unity and courage in the face of adversity.

The Kraken's influence extended beyond European shores. In Far East cultures, similar creatures were described with varying names and attributes. In Japanese folklore, the "Umibōzu" was said to be a giant sea spirit capable of capsizing ships and drowning sailors. China had its own tales of colossal sea monsters, often depicted as dragons or serpents with the ability to create devastating tidal waves. These legends mirrored the respect and awe that coastal communities held for the powerful seas.

As the world became more interconnected through trade and exploration, the Kraken's legend seeped into popular literature and art. Authors like Jules Verne and Alfred Tennyson referenced the Kraken in their works, perpetuating its iconic status in the literary realm. In the 20th and 21st centuries, the

THE KRAKEN QUEST: EXPLORING THE MYTHICAL GIANTS OF THE SEA

Kraken continued to inspire creativity, appearing in numerous films, video games, and fantasy novels. Its enduring presence in modern culture is a testament to its enduring fascination as a symbol of mystery and the unknown depths of the ocean.

The Kraken, a creature born from the depths of human imagination and maritime experiences, has left an indelible mark on different civilizations throughout history. From the ancient Norse seafarers to modern-day pop culture, the Kraken's legend persists, representing the vastness, dangers, and allure of the sea. As we continue on "The Kraken Quest: Exploring the Mythical Giants of the Sea," we will venture further into the realms of mystery and delve into the various depictions of this awe-inspiring creature in different cultures and time periods.

The early myths and documented encounters surrounding the Kraken are shrouded in a mix of folklore, superstition, and genuine attempts to understand the mysterious phenomena witnessed at sea. As maritime exploration and trade expanded in the medieval era, sailors and explorers encountered various sea creatures and phenomena that they struggled to explain. Among these enigmatic encounters emerged the legends and tales of the Kraken, a creature that would go on to captivate the imagination of generations.

Among the earliest references to the Kraken can be found in the sagas of the Viking Age. These Norse texts, written in Old Norse during the 13th century, described the Kraken as a colossal sea monster dwelling off the coasts of Norway and Greenland. It was depicted as a terrifying creature with massive tentacles that could drag entire ships and crew beneath the waves. The sagas spoke of the creature's ability to create deadly whirlpools and bring forth storms, reinforcing the belief in its formidable power.

In 1539, Olaus Magnus, a Swedish historian and cartographer, published the "Carta Marina," a detailed map of Northern Europe and the North Atlantic. Among the many illustrations on the map, one caught the attention of many: a monstrous creature named "Hafgufa." This creature bore a striking resemblance to the Kraken, described as an immense sea serpent capable of swallowing ships whole. Olaus Magnus's map solidified the Kraken's place in European folklore and fueled curiosity about the mysteries lurking beneath the ocean's surface.

In 1752, Danish bishop Erik Pontoppidan published "The Natural History of Norway," a comprehensive work that included accounts of strange sea creatures, including the Kraken. Pontoppidan collected various tales from sailors and fishermen, who described their encounters with the Kraken in chilling detail. His work served as a significant source for early maritime legends, making the Kraken more widely known beyond Scandinavia.

During the Age of Sail, sailors frequently etched images on whalebone or ivory, known as scrimshaw, during their long journeys at sea. Many of these engravings featured depictions of sea monsters, including the Kraken, which reflected their fears and experiences while sailing through uncharted waters. Sailors' tales of witnessing giant tentacles rising from the

THE KRAKEN QUEST: EXPLORING THE MYTHICAL GIANTS OF THE SEA

depths and dragging ships beneath the waves added to the lore of the Kraken and perpetuated its mystique.

The Kraken found its way into various literary works during the 19th century. Authors like Alfred Tennyson in his famous poem "The Kraken" and Jules Verne in his novel "Twenty Thousand Leagues Under the Sea" further popularized the creature's legend. These literary portrayals often blended the mythical aspects of the Kraken with scientific speculations about undiscovered sea creatures.

The Kraken's early myths likely stem from ancient Norse and other seafaring cultures' encounters with giant cephalopods like the colossal squid and the giant squid. These real-life creatures, with their enormous size and mysterious habits, might have served as the inspiration for the Kraken myth. The Kraken's symbolism as a representation of the untamed, uncontrollable forces of the sea reinforced the belief that the oceans held uncharted territories filled with danger and wonder.

The Kraken's early myths and documented encounters emerged from the experiences and imaginations of seafaring cultures throughout history. From the sagas of the Vikings to the maritime adventures of explorers and sailors, the Kraken's legend evolved and spread across different regions. While the tales might have been embellished over time, they reflect humanity's enduring fascination with the unknown and the profound mysteries that lie beneath the surface of the vast and unpredictable oceans. As we continue our quest to explore the mythical giants of the sea in "The Kraken Quest," we will further investigate the scientific inquiries and modern interpretations of this legendary sea creature.

The Kraken, as a legendary sea monster, has fascinated people for centuries. While the creature's existence as a colossal, tentacled behemoth remains firmly in the realm of mythology and folklore, there are scientific explanations and potential real-life inspirations behind the Kraken legends.

One of the most plausible real-life inspirations for the Kraken legends lies in the world of giant cephalopods. The colossal squid (Mesonychoteuthis hamiltoni) and the giant squid (Architeuthis dux) are two such species. These deep-sea creatures, dwelling in the ocean's depths, have rarely been observed alive, leading to their elusive and mysterious nature. Ancient sailors and seafarers might have encountered the remains of these massive cephalopods washed ashore, giving rise to tales of sea monsters with enormous tentacles.

The size and appearance of giant cephalopods could have been exaggerated over time, leading to the creation of the monstrous Kraken in folklore. The Kraken's ability to drag ships under the water might have been inspired by observations of these giant creatures entangling their prey with their long tentacles.

The Kraken's legend could also be tied to observations of epic battles between sperm whales and giant squids. Sperm whales are known to dive to great depths in search of prey, and giant squids are one of their main food sources. Encounters between these two colossal creatures might have been witnessed by sailors and passed down as tales of epic sea battles. The sight of a massive squid's tentacles thrashing in the water as it fought against a massive whale could have easily given rise to stories of a sea monster capable of toppling ships.

Reports of the Kraken's ability to create deadly whirlpools and underwater turbulence could have been inspired by real-life ocean phenomena. Whirlpools and powerful currents are known to occur in various regions of the world's oceans due to the interaction of tides, currents, and underwater topography. Ancient mariners might have encountered these natural phenomena and attributed them to the actions of a mythical sea creature like the Kraken.

In the era before extensive scientific knowledge and global exploration, sailors encountered numerous marine creatures that were unfamiliar to them. The sighting of large, bizarre, or rare creatures might have been misinterpreted or embellished, contributing to the development of the Kraken legends. Sea serpents and other mythical marine beings were often described based on limited and unreliable observations, further adding to the maritime lore.

The Kraken legends, while rooted in mythology and imagination, have potential real-life inspirations and scientific explanations. Observations of giant cephalopods like the colossal squid and giant squid, as well as encounters between sperm whales and squids, could have played a role in the creation of the Kraken's myth. Additionally, natural ocean phenomena, misidentifications of marine creatures, and a lack of scientific understanding might have contributed to the stories of the Kraken's fearsome abilities.

As we continue "The Kraken Quest: Exploring the Mythical Giants of the Sea," we will further investigate the diverse interpretations of the Kraken in different cultures and delve into the enduring impact of this legendary sea monster on popular culture and human imagination.

Chapter 2: Anatomy of the Kraken

Throughout history, the Kraken has been depicted in various ways in folklore, mythology, and literature. Its appearance and abilities have evolved and expanded over time as the legend of this mythical sea creature spread across different cultures and literary works.

In almost all accounts, the Kraken is portrayed as an enormous creature of immense size, often surpassing the dimensions of the largest sea vessels. Descriptions vary from the creature being as large as a small island to having tentacles stretching for miles. This gargantuan scale emphasizes the Kraken's status as a behemoth of the deep, striking fear into the hearts of sailors and coastal dwellers.

One of the most iconic features of the Kraken is its many tentacles. These appendages are described as long, powerful, and capable of reaching great distances. The number of tentacles varies across different tales, ranging from the traditional depiction of eight tentacles to more extravagant descriptions with dozens of limbs. The Kraken's tentacles are often portrayed as flexible and capable of entangling ships or dragging entire vessels beneath the waves.

The Kraken is often associated with the depths of the ocean, residing in the darkest and most mysterious regions of the sea. Its home is believed to be in underwater caves or deep trenches, emerging only to terrorize sailors or prey on unfortunate creatures that wander too close to its domain. This association with the deep ocean adds to the creature's enigmatic nature and the sense of the unknown lurking beneath the waves.

The Kraken is frequently attributed with the power to create strong whirlpools, vortexes, and powerful tidal currents. These abilities are believed to be responsible for ships mysteriously disappearing and sailors meeting their doom at sea. The Kraken's control over the waters serves to heighten its danger and reinforce its role as a fearsome force of nature.

In some accounts, the Kraken is described as a creature that can disappear beneath the waves as quickly as it emerges. Its ability to blend in with the ocean's surface makes it difficult to spot until it strikes. This element of stealth adds an air of unpredictability and menace to the Kraken's character.

The Kraken is consistently depicted as a destructive force, capable of wreaking havoc on ships, coastal communities, and even entire coastlines. Its immense power is often attributed to its size, strength, and mysterious abilities. The fear of the Kraken's destructive potential served as a cautionary tale for sailors, warning them of the dangers that awaited them on their voyages.

Beyond its physical attributes and abilities, the Kraken also holds symbolic significance. It represents the vastness of the unexplored oceans and the unknown mysteries of the deep. The Kraken embodies the untamed power of nature, reminding humans of their vulnerability and the uncontrollable forces that govern the sea.

THE KRAKEN QUEST: EXPLORING THE MYTHICAL GIANTS OF THE SEA

The descriptions of the Kraken's appearance and abilities in folklore and literature are diverse, reflecting the rich tapestry of human imagination and the maritime cultures that birthed this legendary sea monster. From its gigantic size and numerous tentacles to its deep-sea dwelling and destructive nature, the Kraken embodies the awe and fear inspired by the vast oceans and the enigmatic creatures that might inhabit them.

As we continue our quest to explore the Kraken's mysteries in "The Kraken Quest," we will delve deeper into the cultural significance and enduring legacy of this mythical giant of the sea.

In modern marine biology studies, researchers have explored the possibility of real-life inspirations for the Kraken legends and investigated various marine organisms to better understand the mythical creature's physiology. While the Kraken remains a legendary sea monster in folklore, these scientific inquiries have shed light on intriguing marine organisms that share some characteristics with the mythical creature.

Comparisons between the Kraken and real-life giant squids (Architeuthis dux) and colossal squids (Mesonychoteuthis hamiltoni) have been prominent in modern marine biology. These cephalopods are among the largest known invertebrates and inhabit the deep ocean. They possess elongated bodies and long tentacles armed with powerful suction cups and hooks. While the Kraken's proportions in folklore might be exaggerated, giant squids and colossal squids exhibit some similarities with the mythical creature's tentacled appearance.

Modern marine biology studies have also focused on the incredible diversity of deep-sea cephalopods, many of which possess bioluminescent properties. Some species of deep-sea squids and octopuses have specialized light-producing organs that they use for communication, camouflage, and attracting prey. This characteristic has been suggested as a potential source of inspiration for the glowing eyes and luminous aura often associated with the Kraken in folklore.

Octopuses are known for their remarkable camouflage abilities, rapidly changing the color and texture of their skin to blend in with their surroundings. This aspect of octopus behavior has been likened to the Kraken's ability to disappear beneath the waves, as described in some legends. While octopuses are considerably smaller than the mythical Kraken, they have sparked comparisons due to their remarkable adaptability and stealth.

Modern marine biology studies emphasize the vastness and complexity of deep-sea ecosystems, where numerous species remain undiscovered or poorly understood. The mysterious nature of these uncharted depths mirrors the sense of the unknown that the Kraken embodies in folklore. Scientists acknowledge that there could still be large marine organisms waiting to be discovered, sparking curiosity about potential real-life inspirations for legendary creatures like the Kraken.

It is important to note that while marine biology studies explore potential real-life inspirations for the Kraken, the creature's existence as depicted in folklore remains firmly in the realm of mythology. Cryptozoology, a field that investigates animals and creatures with limited or disputed evidence, has delved into the study of legendary creatures like the Kraken. However, most scientific communities remain skeptical about the existence of mythical beings and emphasize the need for empirical evidence to substantiate such claims.

Modern marine biology studies have allowed scientists to draw interesting comparisons between the Kraken's mythical characteristics and real-life marine organisms. Giant squids, deep-sea cephalopods, octopuses, and the mysteries of unexplored deep-sea ecosystems have all contributed to discussions about potential inspirations for the Kraken's physiology.

However, it is essential to recognize the distinction between folklore and scientific investigation. The Kraken remains a fascinating creature of the human imagination, continuing to captivate minds with its legendary status in the rich tapestry of maritime myths and stories.

As we continue on "The Kraken Quest: Exploring the Mythical Giants of the Sea," we will further explore the cultural significance of the Kraken and its enduring impact on human imagination and popular culture, even as modern science continues to unravel the mysteries of the real marine world.

As a mythical creature, the Kraken's survival in the extreme depths of the ocean is a subject of imaginative speculation rather than scientific analysis. However, based on the characteristics attributed to the Kraken in folklore and modern marine biology insights, we can explore hypothetical adaptations that such a creature might possess to survive in the deep ocean:

1. Bioluminescence: Like many deep-sea organisms, the Kraken could possess bioluminescent capabilities. Bioluminescence would allow the creature to produce light and potentially use it for communication, attracting prey, or intimidating predators in the pitch-black depths.

2. Camouflage and Transparency: To blend seamlessly with its environment, the Kraken might have evolved camouflage mechanisms, similar to modern cephalopods like the octopus and cuttlefish. It could rapidly change its skin color, pattern, and texture to remain virtually invisible to potential threats or prey.

3. Gigantic Size and Muscular Strength: To survive in the immense pressure of the deep ocean, the Kraken might have a robust and sturdy body structure. Its large size could provide the necessary buoyancy to navigate and endure the crushing depths, while its muscular strength would aid in capturing prey or fending off predators.

4. Adapted Vision: In the darkness of the deep ocean, the Kraken could have specialized eyes capable of detecting faint light or sensing movement in low-light conditions. It might also have developed heightened sensitivity to bioluminescent signals in the pitch-black environment.

5. Slow Metabolism: The Kraken could have a slow metabolism to conserve energy in the nutrient-poor deep-sea environment. Such an adaptation would enable it to survive on minimal food

resources for extended periods, waiting for suitable prey to pass by.

6. Large Tentacles and Feeding Mechanisms: The Kraken's massive tentacles, like those of real-life giant squids and colossal squids, could be adapted for efficient hunting and feeding. Powerful suction cups and sharp hooks might allow the Kraken to capture and subdue prey effortlessly.

7. Pressure Resistance: To survive in the extreme pressure of the deep ocean, the Kraken might have developed specialized adaptations in its body tissues, such as strong proteins or flexible membranes, to withstand the crushing forces of the water at great depths.

8. Slow Metabolic Waste Production: In the deep ocean, waste breakdown and nutrient recycling are slow processes. The Kraken could have evolved to produce minimal metabolic waste or efficiently recycle its waste to maintain a sustainable ecosystem within its body.

It is crucial to reiterate that the Kraken is a mythical creature, and any discussion of its adaptations is purely speculative and imaginative. While many of the characteristics mentioned above align with real-life deep-sea organisms, the Kraken remains firmly rooted in folklore and maritime legends. The mysteries of the deep ocean continue to fascinate and inspire human imagination, giving rise to legendary creatures like the Kraken in the rich tapestry of myths and stories.

EDWARD TURNER

Chapter 3: Natural History and Evolution

The evolutionary history of cephalopods is a fascinating journey that spans hundreds of millions of years. These enigmatic creatures belong to the phylum Mollusca, class Cephalopoda, and have a lineage rich in diversity and complexity. While cephalopods do not have a direct connection to the mythical Kraken, studying their evolutionary history can provide insights into the potential inspirations for the legendary sea monster.

The earliest cephalopods appeared during the Late Cambrian period, approximately 500 million years ago. These early cephalopods, known as orthocerids and nautiloids, were primitive and primarily had straight shells. They thrived in ancient oceans and evolved diverse shapes and sizes during the Paleozoic era. The nautiloids, represented today by the chambered nautilus, are the only lineage that survived from this ancient time to the present day.

During the Mesozoic era, specifically in the Paleozoic and Jurassic periods (approximately 200 to 65 million years ago), ammonoids, a subclass of cephalopods, flourished. Ammonoids, such as ammonites, were marine animals with spiral shells and inhabited various marine environments worldwide. Ammonites were highly successful and exhibited a remarkable array of shell shapes, making them essential index fossils for dating geological strata.

With the extinction of ammonites at the end of the Cretaceous period, modern cephalopods began to diversify during the Cenozoic era (approximately 65 million years ago to the present). This period saw the emergence of two main groups of modern cephalopods: squids (subclass Coleoidea) and octopuses (order Octopoda).

Squids: Modern squids, such as the giant squid (Architeuthis) and colossal squid (Mesonychoteuthis), are believed to be the closest living relatives to the ancient ammonoids. Their soft-bodied nature makes them challenging to fossilize, leading to limited direct evidence of their evolutionary history. However, their body structure, tentacled appearance, and large size have sparked comparisons with the Kraken in folklore and popular culture.

Octopuses: Octopuses, on the other hand, are not as closely linked to the Kraken's potential inspiration due to their lack of shells and predominantly solitary behavior. Their appearance and behavior are quite distinct from the traditional depictions of the Kraken in legends.

While modern cephalopods have intriguing characteristics that could have influenced the Kraken legends, it is important to remember that the Kraken is a mythical creature. The stories of the Kraken likely evolved from a combination of real-life encounters with large marine animals, such as giant squids or colossal squids, and the fertile imaginations of seafarers and storytellers. As such, the connection between cephalopods and the Kraken is rooted in folklore, myth, and the enduring fascination with the mysteries of the deep sea.

The evolutionary history of cephalopods showcases their remarkable diversification and adaptation over millions of years. From the ancient nautiloids and ammonites to the modern squids and octopuses, these creatures have left an indelible mark on Earth's biological history. While modern cephalopods have intriguing characteristics that align with some aspects of the Kraken legends, the connection between cephalopods and the mythical sea monster is rooted in human imagination and the enduring allure of maritime myths and stories.

Giant cephalopods, such as the ancient nautiloids and ammonites during the Paleozoic and Mesozoic eras, played significant ecological roles in prehistoric marine ecosystems. These enigmatic creatures were among the dominant marine predators of their time and occupied various niches in the ancient oceans.

Giant cephalopods were apex predators, meaning they held the highest position in the food chain. With their formidable size, strength, and tentacled arms armed with sharp hooks, they were efficient hunters capable of capturing and subduing a wide range of prey. Their diet likely included smaller marine organisms such as fish, crustaceans, and other cephalopods. As apex predators, they exerted top-down control on the marine food web, regulating the abundance and distribution of other marine species.

Certain giant cephalopods, such as ammonites, were prolific shell-formers. Their intricate and chambered shells provided essential habitats for various marine organisms. As these cephalopods died, their shells accumulated on the ocean floor, creating rich substrate environments that other organisms could colonize. Ammonite shells also contributed to the formation of limestone deposits, influencing sedimentation patterns and altering marine ecosystems.

While giant cephalopods were apex predators, they were not invincible. They themselves were preyed upon by various marine reptiles and large fish, such as ichthyosaurs, plesiosaurs, and predatory sharks. This interaction created a dynamic balance in the prehistoric marine ecosystems, where predation and predation avoidance shaped the population dynamics of these organisms.

Giant cephalopods, as apex predators, had a cascading effect on the marine food web. Their predation on certain species could influence the abundance of lower trophic levels, causing shifts in community structure and species composition. Trophic cascades, in which changes in the abundance of one species impact multiple trophic levels, would have been evident in prehistoric marine ecosystems due to the presence of giant cephalopods.

The activity of giant cephalopods, particularly when they burrowed into sediment or disturbed the seafloor in search of prey, contributed to bioturbation. Bioturbation involves the physical disruption of sediment layers, which enhances nutrient cycling and promotes the exchange of oxygen and other essential compounds between the water and sediment. This process benefited benthic communities and influenced local ecological dynamics.

Giant cephalopods served as indicator species, reflecting the health and dynamics of prehistoric marine ecosystems. Changes in their population sizes, distributions, or extinction events could signal shifts in environmental conditions, predator-prey relationships, or oceanic currents. As indicator species, they offered insights into the overall health and stability of ancient marine ecosystems.

Giant cephalopods held vital ecological roles in prehistoric marine ecosystems, acting as apex predators, ecological engineers, and key players in trophic cascades. Their interactions with other marine organisms shaped the structure and function of ancient marine food webs. While the giant cephalopods of the past have long since disappeared, their ecological legacy can be glimpsed in the fossil records and provides valuable insights into the dynamic and diverse nature of prehistoric marine life.

Currently there is no conclusive evidence of modern-day colossal cephalopods that match the mythical size attributed to creatures like the Kraken in folklore. However, it is essential to note that the deep ocean remains one of the least explored and understood ecosystems on Earth. Many parts of the deep sea remain unexplored, and new discoveries are continuously being made, which may shed light on the existence of large cephalopods or other mysterious creatures.

That said, there are some fascinating cephalopods in the deep sea that, while not colossal in size, have unique characteristics and play important roles in marine ecosystems:

1. Giant Squid (Architeuthis dux):

The giant squid is one of the largest known cephalopods and has been the subject of intense fascination for centuries. Although not as massive as the mythical Kraken, it can grow up to 43 feet (13 meters) in length. It is known to inhabit the deep ocean and is believed to be an important predator in its environment, preying on fish and other cephalopods. The giant squid remains elusive, and much of what is known about it comes from rare sightings, specimens washed ashore, and the examination of its beaks found in the stomachs of sperm whales.

2. Colossal Squid (Mesonychoteuthis hamiltoni):

The colossal squid is another large cephalopod that dwells in the deep ocean. While not as long as the giant squid, it is believed to have a more massive and robust body, making it one of the heaviest known cephalopods. Colossal squids have large, sharp hooks on their tentacles, likely used for capturing prey. As with the giant squid, much of what is known about the colossal squid comes from rare encounters and studies of specimens.

3. Deep-Sea Octopuses:

Deep-sea octopuses are known for their exceptional adaptability and survival in extreme environments. Some

THE KRAKEN QUEST: EXPLORING THE MYTHICAL GIANTS OF THE SEA

species exhibit unique features, such as bioluminescence, to communicate or camouflage themselves in the dark depths. One example is the Dumbo octopus, named after its ear-like fins, which is found at extreme depths and serves as an important member of the deep-sea ecosystem.

The Impact on Marine Life:

While the existence of colossal cephalopods comparable to the Kraken is speculative and lacks scientific evidence, modern cephalopods, including the giant squid and colossal squid, undoubtedly play vital roles in their deep-sea ecosystems. As apex predators, they are likely essential in regulating prey populations, contributing to the balance of marine food webs.

Additionally, cephalopods, including smaller species like squid and octopuses, serve as prey for various marine organisms, including whales, sharks, and fish. Their abundance and distribution can impact the feeding patterns and dynamics of higher trophic levels in the ocean.

Moreover, cephalopods are known for their rapid growth rates and high reproductive capacities, allowing them to respond quickly to environmental changes. Changes in cephalopod populations could influence the abundance and distribution of their prey and predators, potentially leading to cascading effects on marine ecosystems.

While modern-day colossal cephalopods resembling the mythical Kraken have not been scientifically verified, the deep ocean remains an exciting frontier for marine exploration and discovery. The giant squid, colossal squid, and other deep-sea cephalopods continue to captivate our imaginations and contribute to our understanding of the complexity and biodiversity of the ocean's depths. As research and exploration efforts in the deep sea continue to expand, we may uncover new and fascinating insights into the mysterious world of cephalopods and their impact on marine life.

Chapter 4: Legends and Folktales from Around the World

The Kraken, a legendary sea monster, has captivated the imaginations of people across various cultures and regions throughout history. While the specifics of the Kraken stories may vary from one culture to another, the theme of a colossal sea creature capable of terrorizing sailors and wreaking havoc on ships is a common thread.

In Scandinavian folklore, particularly in Norse mythology, the Kraken is known as a sea monster that terrorizes the waters off the coasts of Norway and Greenland. Descriptions of the Kraken vary, but it is typically depicted as a gigantic cephalopod or sea serpent with long tentacles capable of dragging entire ships beneath the waves. According to these legends, sailors feared encountering the Kraken during their voyages, as it was believed to bring deadly storms and treacherous waters.

The "Carta Marina," a map published by Swedish historian Olaus Magnus in 1539, featured an illustration of a sea monster named "Hafgufa." This creature bears a striking resemblance to the Kraken of Scandinavian folklore and likely influenced the Kraken's image in subsequent tales and literature.

Erik Pontoppidan, a Danish bishop, published "The Natural History of Norway" in 1752. The book included accounts of the Kraken based on reports from sailors and fishermen.

Pontoppidan described the Kraken as a colossal sea creature capable of creating dangerous whirlpools and bringing forth storms. His work contributed to the spread of Kraken stories beyond Scandinavia.

In Greenlandic Inuit mythology, the Qalupalik is a sea creature that shares similarities with the Kraken. The Qalupalik is depicted as a sea-dwelling humanoid creature with long hair and green skin. It is believed to live beneath the sea ice and surfaces to snatch away children who wander too close to the water's edge. The fear of the Qalupalik serves as a cautionary tale to keep children safe from the dangers of the Arctic waters.

Alfred Lord Tennyson, a renowned English poet, immortalized the Kraken in his poem "The Kraken," published in 1830. In the poem, Tennyson describes the Kraken lying in the deep ocean, asleep for centuries. When it awakens, its rise to the surface is accompanied by dramatic natural phenomena, suggesting the creature's immense power and ancient nature.

The Kraken's legend continues to influence modern popular culture, particularly in literature, movies, and video games. It often appears as a colossal sea monster that poses a formidable challenge to sailors and adventurers. Many works of fiction portray the Kraken as an ancient and mythical creature whose existence eludes scientific understanding.

Kraken stories from different cultures and regions share a common fascination with the mysterious and dangerous elements of the ocean. Whether it is the sea serpents of Norse mythology, the Qalupalik of Inuit folklore, or the giant cephalopods of modern fiction, the Kraken's legend continues to evoke awe and fear of the unknown depths of the sea. The enduring appeal of the Kraken in human imagination is a testament to its status as one of the most iconic and enduring sea monsters in maritime mythology.

The Kraken tales from different cultures and regions share several motifs and themes, reflecting the universal human fascination with the mysteries and dangers of the sea. While the specific details of the stories may vary, these common elements contribute to the enduring cultural significance of the Kraken legend:

1. Enigmatic Sea Monster:

Across all cultures, the Kraken is depicted as an enigmatic and colossal sea monster. Its immense size, mysterious nature, and deep-sea dwelling reinforce the idea of the ocean as a realm of uncharted wonders and potential dangers. The Kraken's portrayal as a creature of myth and legend underscores the human fascination with the unknown and the allure of exploring uncharted territories.

2. Sailor's Fear and Cautionary Tales:

In most Kraken stories, sailors are warned of the dangers posed by the mythical sea monster. The tales serve as cautionary warnings, emphasizing the perils of the open ocean and the unpredictability of marine life. Such stories likely served practical purposes, encouraging sailors to exercise caution and navigate treacherous waters safely. They also highlight the psychological impact of facing the vastness and dangers of the sea, an element that has resonated with seafarers throughout history.

3. Control over Nature:

Many Kraken tales ascribe supernatural abilities to the sea monster, such as creating whirlpools, causing storms, and dragging ships beneath the waves. These powers underscore the Kraken's status as a force of nature, beyond human comprehension or control. In such narratives, the Kraken represents the overwhelming power and unpredictability of the natural world, reminding humans of their vulnerability in the face of nature's forces.

4. Symbolism of the Deep:

The Kraken's association with the deep ocean serves as a symbol of the unfathomable depths and hidden wonders that lie beneath the sea's surface. The ocean's vastness and the creatures that inhabit its darkest reaches have historically been a source of awe and curiosity for humans. The Kraken embodies this fascination with the deep sea and the mysteries that it conceals.

5. Cultural Identity and Folklore:

The Kraken's legend is deeply rooted in the maritime cultures of various regions. Stories of the Kraken are woven into the fabric of these cultures, reflecting their dependence on the sea for livelihood, trade, and exploration. By passing down these tales through generations, communities reaffirm their cultural identity and connect with their maritime heritage.

6. Enduring Impact on Popular Culture:

THE KRAKEN QUEST: EXPLORING THE MYTHICAL GIANTS OF THE SEA

The Kraken's cultural significance extends beyond traditional folklore and mythology. Its portrayal in literature, art, and modern popular culture has perpetuated the legend's allure and impact. The Kraken remains an iconic sea monster in literature, movies, and video games, capturing the imaginations of audiences worldwide. Its presence in modern storytelling continues to evoke the themes of adventure, danger, and the unknown, resonating with contemporary audiences as it did with ancient seafarers.

The shared motifs and themes in Kraken tales from different cultures and regions reflect the profound and enduring relationship between humans and the sea. The Kraken's legend represents a cultural fascination with the ocean's mysteries, the dangers of maritime exploration, and the awe-inspiring forces of nature. As a mythical sea monster, the Kraken continues to be an evocative symbol of the vastness and wonders of the deep, perpetuating its cultural significance through generations of storytelling and artistic expression.

The Kraken myth has had a profound influence on maritime cultures and superstitions throughout history. Its legend has shaped the beliefs, practices, and fears of seafarers, fostering a sense of mystery and caution about the vast and unpredictable oceans.

The Kraken's depiction as a colossal and mysterious sea monster has instilled a deep fear of the unknown in sailors and maritime communities. The vastness of the ocean and the uncertainties it holds have been a source of trepidation for seafarers throughout history. The Kraken myth reinforced the idea of the ocean as a realm of uncharted wonders and potential dangers, heightening the sailors' sense of vulnerability and inspiring caution in their maritime endeavors.

Kraken myths served as cautionary tales, warning sailors about the perils of the open sea. They often emphasized the importance of following maritime superstitions and practices to appease the spirits and deities associated with the ocean. Sailors would engage in rituals, such as making offerings or avoiding certain actions, to avoid provoking the wrath of the Kraken or other sea monsters. These superstitions were believed to bring luck, protection, and safe voyages.

The Kraken's legend has left a significant impact on nautical art, literature, and cartography. Artists, writers, and cartographers often incorporated depictions of the Kraken in their works, adding an element of mystery and danger to maritime tales. The imagery of the Kraken in maps, paintings, and literature reinforced the idea of a world full of uncharted territories and potential dangers, encouraging exploration and curiosity.

Kraken myths have become an integral part of maritime cultures, shaping their cultural identity and folklore. These stories have been passed down through generations, connecting communities with their maritime heritage and fostering a sense of shared identity among seafarers. The tales of the Kraken have become woven into the fabric of maritime societies, reflecting their unique relationship with the sea and its many mysteries.

THE KRAKEN QUEST: EXPLORING THE MYTHICAL GIANTS OF THE SEA

The belief in sea monsters like the Kraken could have significant psychological effects on sailors. The fear of encountering such mythical creatures, along with the harsh realities of life at sea, might have led to anxiety and apprehension during long voyages. Sailors would share tales of their experiences and beliefs in sea monsters during their time at sea, reinforcing the cultural significance of Kraken myths and superstitions within the maritime community.

The influence of Kraken myths extends beyond historical maritime cultures. The legend of the Kraken continues to resonate in modern popular culture, with appearances in literature, movies, and video games. These contemporary interpretations of the Kraken keep the mythical sea monster alive in the collective imagination and maintain its impact on human fascination with the sea and its mysteries.

The Kraken myth has left a lasting mark on maritime cultures and superstitions, shaping beliefs, practices, and psychological perspectives of seafarers. Its portrayal as a colossal and mysterious sea monster has instilled a sense of awe and fear about the unknown depths of the ocean, driving sailors to embrace maritime superstitions and rituals for protection and safe voyages. The Kraken's legend has become an integral part of maritime folklore and cultural identity, continuing to inspire curiosity, caution, and fascination with the enigmatic world of the sea.

EDWARD TURNER

42

Chapter 5: Kraken in Art and Literature

The representation of the Kraken in art spans centuries and has evolved over time, reflecting changes in artistic styles, cultural beliefs, and storytelling techniques. Both ancient and contemporary art have depicted the mythical sea monster in various forms, showcasing the enduring fascination with the legendary creature.

Ancient Art:

1. Maps and Cartography:

In medieval and Renaissance maps, sea monsters, including the Kraken, were often depicted in uncharted waters as warnings to sailors about potential dangers. These maps featured fantastical illustrations of the Kraken rising from the depths, engaging in battle with ships, or creating whirlpools. Notable examples include the "Carta Marina" by Olaus Magnus (1539) and the "Hic sunt dracones" ("Here be dragons") notation on old maps.

2. Sculptures and Carvings:

In ancient maritime cultures, sculptures and carvings of sea creatures, including the Kraken, adorned ship prows and maritime buildings. These sculptures were often meant to invoke protection and good fortune during voyages. Ancient cultures, such as the Vikings, incorporated Kraken-like sea monsters into their artistic expressions to emphasize the sea's inherent dangers and the need for divine protection.

Contemporary Art:

1. Paintings and Illustrations:

In contemporary art, the Kraken continues to be a popular subject for painters and illustrators. Modern artists often depict the Kraken in highly detailed and realistic illustrations, reflecting the creature's awe-inspiring presence and its mythological roots. Paintings and digital art pieces often portray the Kraken in dramatic scenes, battling ships or lurking beneath the waves.

2. Literature and Book Covers:

With the enduring popularity of Kraken myths in literature, book covers often feature artistic renditions of the creature. Whether it is classic literature, fantasy novels, or children's books, the Kraken's presence on book covers invokes a sense of adventure and mystery, drawing readers into the depths of the story.

3. Sculptures and Installations:

Contemporary sculptors have also embraced the Kraken as a subject for their artistic creations. Sculptures, both large-scale installations and smaller art pieces, have been crafted to capture the Kraken's elusive and monstrous nature. These sculptures often emphasize the creature's tentacles and imposing size, creating striking visual representations.

THE KRAKEN QUEST: EXPLORING THE MYTHICAL GIANTS OF THE SEA

4. Video Games and Digital Media:

The Kraken has become an iconic figure in video games and digital media. From colossal boss battles in action-adventure games to fantastical depictions in fantasy RPGs, the Kraken's legend has inspired game designers and digital artists to create awe-inspiring and terrifying versions of the sea monster.

The representation of the Kraken in ancient and contemporary art reflects the enduring appeal and cultural significance of the mythical sea monster. Ancient maps and sculptures captured the fears and uncertainties of sailors in uncharted waters, while contemporary art continues to captivate audiences with its imaginative and awe-inspiring portrayals of the Kraken. From the engravings on historical maps to the digital art of modern video games, the Kraken's legend continues to inspire artists and storytellers, making it an iconic and enduring figure in the world of art and popular culture.

Several famous literary works have featured the Kraken, further solidifying its status as an iconic sea monster in popular culture. These works have contributed to the enduring fascination with the mythical creature and have inspired countless adaptations, references, and retellings in various forms of media. Let's analyze some of these significant literary works and their impact on popular culture:

1. Alfred Lord Tennyson's Poem "The Kraken" (1830):

Tennyson's poem "The Kraken" is one of the earliest and most influential literary works centered around the legendary sea monster. The poem vividly describes the Kraken lying in the depths of the ocean, slumbering for centuries, and awakening with tremendous power when it finally rises to the surface. Tennyson's lyrical and evocative language captures the awe and mystery of the deep sea, elevating the Kraken to an emblematic symbol of the ocean's enigmatic wonders. "The Kraken" has served as a source of inspiration for subsequent writers, artists, and filmmakers, keeping the creature's legend alive in the literary canon.

2. Jules Verne's Novel "20,000 Leagues Under the Sea" (1870):

In Verne's classic science fiction novel, "20,000 Leagues Under the Sea," the Kraken is referenced as one of the legendary sea monsters encountered by Captain Nemo and the crew of the submarine Nautilus. While the Kraken does not play a central role in the plot, its inclusion adds an element of mystery and danger to the unexplored depths that the characters traverse. Verne's novel popularized the concept of deep-sea exploration and maritime adventure, further fueling public fascination with sea monsters and the mysteries of the ocean.

3. H.P. Lovecraft's Short Story "The Call of Cthulhu" (1928):

While not explicitly referred to as the Kraken, Lovecraft's cosmic horror tale "The Call of Cthulhu" introduced a monstrous deity known as Cthulhu, which shares thematic and visual similarities with the Kraken. Cthulhu, an ancient, tentacled, and otherworldly entity, lies dormant beneath the sea, waiting for the right moment to rise and wreak havoc upon the world. Lovecraft's creation has become an iconic figure in horror literature and has inspired a vast and enduring mythos known as the Cthulhu Mythos. The themes of ancient cosmic horrors and the vastness of the unknown in Lovecraft's work resonate with the Kraken's legend and have contributed to the enduring popularity of both creatures in popular culture.

4. Rick Riordan's "Percy Jackson & the Olympians" Series (2005-2009):

In the modern young adult fantasy series by Rick Riordan, the Kraken makes an appearance as a formidable sea monster controlled by the sea god Poseidon. Riordan's depiction of the Kraken showcases its monstrous and dangerous qualities, reflecting the creature's role in maritime mythology. The "Percy Jackson & the Olympians" series has introduced young readers to the rich tapestry of Greek mythology, including legendary creatures like the Kraken, and has further ingrained its image in contemporary popular culture.

The presence of the Kraken in these and other literary works has had a profound impact on popular culture. Its portrayal as a colossal and enigmatic sea monster continues to captivate imaginations and serves as a source of inspiration for various forms of media. The Kraken's legend has been embraced and reimagined in numerous novels, films, television shows, video games, and art pieces.

The creature's representation in popular culture has contributed to its status as an enduring and iconic figure in maritime mythology. Its imagery has become synonymous with the mysteries of the ocean, the perils of seafaring, and the allure of exploration. As a result, the Kraken remains an essential component of the collective imagination, with its legend continuing to inspire new generations of creators and storytellers in their portrayal of the deep and the mythical sea monsters that dwell within it.

The Kraken, as a legendary sea monster, has been a rich source of inspiration for artists, writers, and filmmakers throughout history. Its enigmatic and terrifying nature, combined with its association with the mysteries of the deep sea, has captured the imaginations of creators in various fields.

The Kraken's depiction in ancient maps, carvings, and sculptures laid the foundation for its representation in art. In medieval and Renaissance maps, sea monsters, including the Kraken, were depicted in uncharted waters as warnings to sailors about potential dangers. Artists, influenced by these maps and maritime folklore, created imaginative illustrations of the Kraken rising from the depths, battling ships, or creating whirlpools. These representations added an element of mystery and danger to maritime art and reflected the fascination with the unknown and the dangers of the sea.

Kraken myths have been featured in various literary works, from epic poems to classic novels and contemporary fiction. The Kraken has appeared in poems such as Alfred Lord Tennyson's "The Kraken," where it is described as an ancient and powerful sea creature. Jules Verne's "20,000 Leagues Under the Sea" and Herman Melville's "Moby-Dick" reference sea monsters, including the Kraken, as part of the maritime adventures in their novels. These literary works have contributed to the enduring popularity of the Kraken legend and its association with maritime exploration and adventure.

The Kraken's legend has been adapted to the silver screen in numerous films, where its terrifying and monstrous qualities are brought to life with visual effects. From classic monster movies to modern fantasy and science fiction films, the Kraken has appeared in various cinematic adaptations. Ray Harryhausen's stop-motion animation brought the Kraken to life in the 1981 film "Clash of the Titans," cementing its place as an iconic movie monster. Additionally, contemporary franchises like "Pirates of the Caribbean" and "Percy Jackson & the Olympians" have featured the Kraken as a formidable sea creature, captivating audiences with its on-screen presence.

Beyond its representation in specific works, the Kraken has become a symbol of fantasy and mythology, permeating a wide range of media and creative endeavors. It continues to appear in fantasy novels, tabletop games, video games, and comic books. Its enduring appeal as a monstrous and awe-inspiring creature is evident in its inclusion in various mythological universes and imaginative storytelling.

The Kraken's presence in popular culture extends beyond its traditional representations in art, literature, and cinema. It has become a recognizable figure in logos, merchandise, and marketing campaigns. The creature's imagery is frequently utilized in sea-themed attractions and events, drawing on its association with maritime myths and legends to evoke a sense of adventure and wonder.

The Kraken's legend has been a wellspring of inspiration for artists, writers, and filmmakers throughout history. Its portrayal in art, literature, and cinema has contributed to its enduring popularity and cultural significance. The Kraken's association with the mysteries of the deep sea, the perils of maritime exploration, and the allure of adventure has resonated with audiences across generations. As a result, the Kraken remains an iconic and enduring figure in the collective imagination, inspiring new generations of creators and continuing to captivate audiences worldwide.

THE KRAKEN QUEST: EXPLORING THE MYTHICAL GIANTS OF THE SEA

51

Chapter 6: The Hunt for the Kraken

Historical attempts to capture or study the Kraken have been shrouded in mystery and folklore, reflecting the fascination and fear surrounding the legendary sea monster. While there are no documented instances of successful captures or scientific studies of the Kraken, historical records reveal various endeavors by sailors, scientists, and naturalists to understand the enigmatic creature.

In the age of exploration and seafaring, sailors reported encounters with large sea creatures that might have been interpreted as the Kraken. These accounts were often recorded in nautical logs and maps, describing massive tentacled creatures attacking ships or creating dangerous whirlpools. However, these reports were likely influenced by the sailors' superstitions and imaginations, with real-world encounters likely involving known marine animals like giant squids.

Erik Pontoppidan, a Danish bishop, compiled "The Natural History of Norway" in 1752, which included descriptions of the Kraken based on reports from sailors and fishermen. Pontoppidan described the Kraken as a colossal sea creature capable of creating dangerous whirlpools and bringing forth storms. Although his work contributed to the spread of Kraken stories beyond Scandinavia, it was a mixture of folklore, mythology, and genuine accounts.

In the 19th and early 20th centuries, giant squids (Architeuthis) started to wash ashore or be found in the stomachs of sperm whales. These encounters provided some evidence of the existence of large cephalopods in the deep sea, lending a degree of credibility to the stories of sea monsters like the Kraken. However, these findings did not confirm the existence of a mythical sea monster but rather revealed real creatures of remarkable size.

Throughout the 20th century, cryptozoologists, researchers who study hidden or undiscovered animals, have explored the possibility of undiscovered marine creatures, including the Kraken. However, these expeditions have yielded little concrete evidence, and their findings often fall into the realm of speculation and conjecture.

With advancements in marine biology and deep-sea exploration technology, scientists have gained a better understanding of the ocean's depths and its inhabitants. Although researchers have discovered new and bizarre creatures, including giant squid, no evidence has been found to support the existence of a colossal, mythological Kraken as described in folklore.

Historical attempts to capture or study the Kraken have been influenced by folklore, nautical tales, and a desire to explore the mysteries of the deep sea. While there have been genuine encounters with large sea creatures like giant squids, the existence of a mythical Kraken with supernatural powers remains unconfirmed. Modern marine biology studies have shed light on the deep ocean's biodiversity, but the Kraken's legend remains firmly rooted in mythology and human imagination. As a result, the Kraken continues to be a captivating symbol of the ocean's enigmatic wonders and the enduring allure of maritime myths and legends.

There have been several famous expeditions and findings related to giant cephalopods, particularly the giant squid (Architeuthis dux). These expeditions have provided valuable insights into the biology, behavior, and distribution of these elusive deep-sea creatures.

1. Prince of Monaco's Expedition (1914):

In 1914, Prince Albert I of Monaco organized an expedition aboard his research vessel, the "Princesse Alice," to investigate the existence of giant squids. During the expedition, they made an important discovery when they caught a giant squid off the coast of the Canary Islands. This specimen provided the scientific community with the first direct evidence of a giant squid, confirming the existence of these elusive deep-sea creatures.

2. National Geographic's Giant Squid Expedition (2004):

In 2004, the National Geographic Society, in collaboration with the Japanese broadcasting company NHK, launched an ambitious expedition to capture footage of a live giant squid. Using a combination of underwater cameras and bait, they successfully captured the first-ever images of a live giant squid in its natural habitat at depths of up to 2,067 feet (630 meters) off the coast of Japan. This groundbreaking expedition provided invaluable visual documentation of the giant squid's behavior and habitat.

3. The Architeuthis Genome Project (2015):

In 2015, scientists led by the University of Copenhagen and Aarhus University announced the completion of the first-ever sequencing of the giant squid's genome. This landmark project shed light on the genetic makeup and evolutionary history of these mysterious creatures. The findings suggested that the giant squid had a complex genome and shared common ancestors with other cephalopods, offering insights into their evolutionary history and adaptations to the deep-sea environment.

4. The Deep-Sea Exploration Vessel, E/V Nautilus:

The E/V Nautilus, operated by the Ocean Exploration Trust, is an exploration vessel equipped with advanced technology for deep-sea research. It has conducted numerous expeditions in various regions, including the Gulf of Mexico and the Caribbean Sea. During these expeditions, the vessel's remotely operated vehicles (ROVs) have captured rare and stunning footage of giant squid and other deep-sea creatures, contributing to our understanding of their behavior and habitats.

5. The NOAA Okeanos Explorer:

The National Oceanic and Atmospheric Administration's (NOAA) Okeanos Explorer is another prominent exploration vessel dedicated to investigating the deep ocean. The vessel has been involved in numerous expeditions to explore the largely uncharted depths of the ocean, including the investigation of deep-sea habitats where giant squid may reside. While not specifically focused on giant cephalopods, these expeditions have contributed to our knowledge of the deep-sea ecosystem and the potential habitats of these elusive creatures.

Famous expeditions related to giant cephalopods, particularly the giant squid, have significantly advanced our understanding of these elusive deep-sea creatures. Through direct observations, genetic studies, and advanced technology, researchers have gained valuable insights into the biology, behavior, and distribution of giant squids. These findings have not only expanded our knowledge of these enigmatic creatures but also sparked further interest in deep-sea exploration and the mysteries that lie beneath the ocean's surface. As technology continues to advance, future expeditions are likely to unveil even more discoveries, deepening our understanding of the fascinating world of giant cephalopods and their role in the marine ecosystem.

Researching cryptids like the Kraken presents several challenges and ethical considerations that researchers must grapple with. Cryptids are creatures that are rumored or believed to exist based on anecdotal accounts, folklore, or unverified evidence, but have not been scientifically proven to exist.

Challenges:

1. Lack of Scientific Evidence: The primary challenge in researching cryptids like the Kraken is the absence of scientific evidence to support their existence. Many cryptids are based on folklore, myths, and unreliable eyewitness accounts, making it difficult to obtain concrete data for scientific investigation.

2. Resource Allocation: Conducting research expeditions to study cryptids requires significant resources, including funding, specialized equipment, and skilled personnel. Allocating resources to investigate unproven creatures can be a contentious issue, especially when other pressing environmental or conservation research may be underfunded.

3. Methodological Difficulties: Studying cryptids in their natural habitats poses methodological challenges. These creatures are often purported to inhabit remote or inaccessible areas, making it logistically challenging to conduct scientific observations and data collection.

4. Ethical Concerns for Animal Welfare: In cases where cryptids are speculated to be living animals, the potential for capturing or disturbing these creatures raises ethical concerns about animal welfare. Researchers must carefully consider the impact of their actions on the cryptids' natural environment and behavior.

Ethical Considerations:

1. Respect for Indigenous and Local Beliefs: Many cryptids are deeply rooted in the folklore and beliefs of indigenous and local communities. When researching these creatures, it is crucial to approach the subject with cultural sensitivity and

respect for the communities' beliefs, ensuring that research does not undermine or dismiss their cultural heritage.

2. Preventing Harm to Ecosystems: Expeditions aimed at studying cryptids must be conducted in a manner that prioritizes the preservation and protection of the ecosystems in which these creatures are speculated to live. Researchers must consider the potential ecological impacts of their activities, especially in fragile or pristine environments.

3. Responsible Dissemination of Information: Ethical considerations also extend to the dissemination of research findings. Researchers must be transparent about the limitations of their data and avoid sensationalizing or exaggerating claims related to cryptids. Responsible reporting can help prevent the spread of misinformation and ensure the scientific community and the public view the research with appropriate skepticism.

4. Encouraging Critical Thinking: Studying cryptids provides an opportunity to promote critical thinking and scientific literacy. Researchers should use these investigations as opportunities to educate the public about the scientific method, skepticism, and the importance of evidence-based research.

Researching cryptids like the Kraken involves navigating various challenges and ethical considerations. As scientists embark on the exploration of these elusive creatures, they must approach the subject with scientific rigor, cultural sensitivity, and a commitment to preserving the natural environment.

While the possibility of discovering new and unknown species is exciting, responsible research practices are essential to ensure that the scientific community and the public approach the study of cryptids with an appropriate balance of curiosity and skepticism.

THE KRAKEN QUEST: EXPLORING THE MYTHICAL GIANTS OF THE SEA

Chapter 7: The Kraken in Science and Media

Modern scientific explanations for Kraken-like phenomena often center around known marine animals and geological processes. While the Kraken remains a mythical creature, some real-world occurrences and marine organisms might have inspired the legend.

1. Giant Squids (Architeuthis dux):

Giant squids are deep-sea cephalopods that can grow up to 43 feet (13 meters) in length, including their tentacles. These creatures were once considered mythical until the late 19th century when the first scientific evidence of their existence was found. Encounters with giant squids might have inspired the tales of the Kraken. These elusive animals typically dwell in the ocean's depths and are rarely seen, contributing to their mysterious reputation.

2. Colossal Squids (Mesonychoteuthis hamiltoni):

Colossal squids are another species of deep-sea cephalopods that share similarities with giant squids but are even more massive. They can reach lengths of up to 46 feet (14 meters) and possess powerful beaks and tentacles. Like giant squids, colossal squids are rarely observed and could have contributed to the Kraken legend.

3. Sperm Whales (Physeter macrocephalus):

Historical accounts of encounters with the Kraken often mention clashes between the creature and sperm whales. It is now known that sperm whales are known to feed on giant and colossal squids. The battles between these two formidable creatures might have given rise to exaggerated tales of the Kraken's encounters with whales.

4. Whirlpools and Ocean Currents:

Some historical accounts of the Kraken describe its ability to create dangerous whirlpools capable of pulling ships underwater. While not the work of a mythical creature, these descriptions might be based on sailors' experiences with strong ocean currents and whirlpools that can pose serious hazards to ships at sea.

5. Geological Events:

In some instances, the Kraken legend might have been influenced by geological events. Underwater volcanic eruptions, earthquakes, or other seismic activities could create tumultuous waters, leading to reports of sea monsters causing havoc.

6. Misidentification of Marine Animals:

In the past, sightings of large marine animals, such as basking sharks or oarfish, might have been misidentified as Kraken-like creatures due to the limited understanding of marine life and the propensity for storytelling and exaggeration.

THE KRAKEN QUEST: EXPLORING THE MYTHICAL GIANTS OF THE SEA

While the Kraken remains a mythical sea monster, modern scientific explanations for Kraken-like phenomena often point to known marine creatures, geological events, and potential misidentifications. Creatures such as giant squids and colossal squids, along with encounters with sperm whales and underwater volcanic activity, might have contributed to the tales and legends of the Kraken. Understanding the origins of these stories through a scientific lens helps to demystify the Kraken myth while appreciating the enduring fascination and mystery surrounding the enigmatic depths of the ocean.

The Kraken has been a popular and iconic figure in movies, television shows, and video games, with its portrayal varying across different media and adaptations. Its depiction in these forms of entertainment has contributed to its enduring popularity and cultural significance.

Movies:

1. "Clash of the Titans" (1981):

In the classic fantasy film "Clash of the Titans," the Kraken is a massive sea monster unleashed by the gods to punish mortals. This portrayal aligns with the Kraken's mythological roots as a creature summoned by divine forces to wreak havoc upon humans. The stop-motion animation used to create the Kraken's appearance has become iconic, cementing its image in popular culture.

2. "Pirates of the Caribbean: Dead Man's Chest" (2006):

In this blockbuster film, the Kraken is depicted as a monstrous sea creature serving as a servant of the sea goddess Calypso. Its tentacles emerge from the depths to drag unfortunate sailors and ships to their watery demise. This portrayal showcases the Kraken's menacing and destructive nature, further solidifying its image as a formidable and terrifying sea monster.

Television Shows:

1. "Vikings" (2013-2020):

The Kraken is referenced in the historical drama series "Vikings," where it is depicted as a mythical sea monster in Norse folklore. The show incorporates Norse mythology and legends, and the Kraken is mentioned in connection to the mystical and unknown elements of the sea.

2. "Supernatural" (2005-2020):

The Kraken makes an appearance in the popular supernatural drama series "Supernatural." In this context, the Kraken is depicted as a supernatural creature that preys on humans and feeds on their fears. The portrayal of the Kraken as a terrifying and mysterious entity fits well within the show's overarching themes of supernatural phenomena.

Video Games:

1. "God of War" Series:

In the "God of War" video game series, the Kraken is a colossal sea creature and a formidable boss enemy. Players must face the Kraken in epic battles that showcase its immense size and destructive power. This portrayal emphasizes the Kraken's role as a mythical monster embodying the wrath of the sea.

2. "Sea of Thieves":

The Kraken features prominently in the action-adventure video game "Sea of Thieves," where players encounter the creature during their voyages on the high seas. The Kraken's design in the game draws on traditional depictions of the creature as a gigantic tentacled monster, and players must coordinate their efforts to defeat it.

The portrayal of the Kraken in movies, television shows, and video games has showcased its enduring appeal as a mythical sea monster. From classic fantasy films like "Clash of the Titans" to contemporary video games like "Sea of Thieves," the Kraken's depiction has varied but often emphasizes its colossal size, tentacled appearance, and terrifying power. These adaptations draw upon the creature's mythological roots and continue to captivate audiences, reinforcing the Kraken's status as an iconic and timeless figure in popular culture.

The media's representation of the Kraken plays a significant role in shaping public perception of the mythical sea monster. Through movies, television shows, video games, books, and other forms of media, the Kraken's image is presented to a wide audience, influencing how people perceive and understand the creature.

1. Creating Iconic Imagery: The media's representation of the Kraken often creates iconic imagery that becomes deeply ingrained in the public's imagination. Whether it's the

stop-motion animation in "Clash of the Titans" or the CGI-rendered Kraken in "Pirates of the Caribbean," these visual depictions leave a lasting impact and become the go-to mental image when people think of the Kraken. As a result, the Kraken's iconic appearance becomes a part of popular culture, even for those who are not familiar with its mythological origins.

2. Shaping Emotional Associations: The portrayal of the Kraken in media influences how people emotionally connect with the creature. When depicted as a terrifying and monstrous sea monster, the Kraken elicits fear and awe from the audience. On the other hand, portrayals that humanize or give the Kraken more sympathetic characteristics might evoke empathy or intrigue. These emotional associations can affect how the Kraken is perceived and remembered by the public.

3. Influencing Knowledge and Beliefs: For many people, the media serves as a primary source of information and entertainment. As such, their exposure to the Kraken through movies, TV shows, and video games can shape their understanding of the creature's traits, behaviors, and mythical origins. While most audiences recognize the Kraken as a mythical being, the media's portrayal can still influence beliefs about the ocean's mysteries and potential undiscovered creatures.

4. Fostering Interest in Mythology and Folklore: The media's representation of the Kraken can spark interest in mythology and folklore. Audiences exposed to Kraken-related stories may seek out more information about its mythological origins and

other legendary creatures. This can lead to a broader appreciation of cultural traditions and a deeper understanding of the world's diverse mythological narratives.

5. Inspiring Creative Works: The media's portrayal of the Kraken inspires creativity and artistic expressions in various forms. Artists, writers, and game developers draw upon these representations to create new stories, artworks, and adaptations. This perpetuates the Kraken's presence in modern culture and ensures its continued influence on public perception.

6. Influence on Marine Conservation: In some cases, the media's representation of the Kraken and other sea monsters can have a subtle impact on marine conservation efforts. Imagery of mythical sea creatures may evoke a sense of wonder and awe for the ocean's mysteries, prompting some individuals to develop an interest in marine life and conservation issues.

The media's representation of the Kraken significantly influences public perception of the mythical sea monster. Its iconic imagery, emotional associations, and impact on knowledge and beliefs contribute to the creature's enduring popularity in popular culture. The portrayal of the Kraken in movies, TV shows, video games, and other media serves as a gateway to the exploration of mythology, folklore, and creative expressions. Ultimately, the media's depiction of the Kraken shapes how people connect with this legendary creature and the larger world of marine mythology and storytelling.

EDWARD TURNER

Chapter 8: Legendary Sea Monsters Beyond the Kraken

Throughout various cultures and mythologies around the world, there is a rich tapestry of legendary sea creatures that have captured human imagination for centuries. These creatures, often shrouded in mystery and wonder, reflect the cultural beliefs, fears, and fascination with the vast and enigmatic oceans.

1. The Sirens (Greek Mythology):

In Greek mythology, the Sirens were beautiful and seductive sea nymphs who lured sailors to their doom with their enchanting voices and songs. Sailors were unable to resist their allure, leading their ships to crash upon the rocky shores where the Sirens resided.

2. The Kelpie (Scottish Folklore):

The Kelpie is a shape-shifting water horse from Scottish folklore. It often takes the form of a beautiful horse, luring unsuspecting travelers to ride on its back before plunging into the water to drown them. The Kelpie is said to be found near rivers and lochs.

3. The Qalupalik (Inuit Mythology):

In Inuit mythology, the Qalupalik is a sea creature that lives beneath the ice and is known to snatch disobedient children who wander too close to the water's edge. It is described as having green skin, long hair, and clawed hands.

4. The Jengu (African Mythology):

The Jengu is a water spirit in African mythology, specifically found among the Cameroon and Sawa people. Often depicted as a beautiful woman with long hair, the Jengu is believed to bring blessings and prosperity to those who appease her but can also cause misfortune if offended.

5. The Sea Serpent (Various Mythologies):

The Sea Serpent is a common mythical creature found in various cultures worldwide. It is often described as a large, long and serpentine creature that dwells in the deep waters. Tales of sea serpents have appeared in Norse, Chinese, and Native American mythologies, among others.

6. The Sea Dragon (Chinese Mythology):

In Chinese mythology, the Sea Dragon is a powerful and benevolent creature that rules over the oceans and seas. Often associated with the East Sea, the Sea Dragon is revered as a deity that brings prosperity, rainfall, and protection to fishermen and sailors.

7. The Bunyip (Australian Aboriginal Mythology):

The Bunyip is a mythical creature from Australian Aboriginal mythology, said to inhabit swamps, rivers, and billabongs. Descriptions of the Bunyip vary, but it is often depicted as a fearsome creature with a mix of reptilian, mammalian, and bird-like features.

8. The Aspidochelone (Medieval European Folklore):

The Aspidochelone is a legendary sea creature from medieval European folklore. It is often depicted as a gigantic sea turtle or whale, capable of luring sailors with its appearance and singing, only to consume them once they get too close.

These are just a few examples of the many legendary sea creatures found in cultures worldwide. These mythical beings continue to inspire art, literature, and storytelling, reflecting humanity's enduring fascination with the vast and mysterious realms of the oceans.

While each of these sea monsters is unique and originates from different cultures and mythologies, there are some similarities and differences when compared to the Kraken.

1. The Kraken:

The Kraken is a legendary sea monster from Norse mythology, known for its massive size, tentacled appearance, and ability to create dangerous whirlpools. It is often portrayed as a monstrous creature summoned by the gods to punish or challenge mortals. The Kraken's mythology is deeply rooted in Scandinavian folklore and has become a popular figure in modern popular culture.

2. The Sirens:

The Sirens, from Greek mythology, are seductive sea nymphs with enchanting voices and songs. Like the Kraken, they have a connection to the sea and are associated with luring sailors to their doom. However, unlike the Kraken, the Sirens are portrayed as alluring and beautiful beings, using their irresistible songs to entice sailors rather than outright attacking them.

3. The Kelpie:

The Kelpie, from Scottish folklore, is a shape-shifting water horse that dwells near bodies of water. Similar to the Kraken, the Kelpie is associated with danger and death for those who come too close to the water. However, unlike the Kraken, which is often depicted as a sea monster, the Kelpie can take the form of a horse, adding a shape-shifting element to its mythology.

4. The Qalupalik:

The Qalupalik, from Inuit mythology, is a sea creature that preys on disobedient children. Similar to the Kraken's association with peril on the seas, the Qalupalik dwells beneath the icy waters and poses a threat to those who venture too close to the frozen edges. Both creatures are characterized as dangerous entities lurking beneath the water's surface.

5. The Jengu:

The Jengu, from African mythology, is a water spirit associated with rivers and water bodies. It is portrayed as a beautiful woman with benevolent qualities, offering blessings and prosperity to those who appease her. Unlike the Kraken, which is often depicted as a terrifying sea monster, the Jengu has a more positive and protective role in the mythology.

6. The Sea Serpent:

The Sea Serpent is a widespread mythical creature found in various cultures worldwide. It shares some similarities with the Kraken, such as its association with the sea and its colossal size. However, sea serpents are often depicted as elongated, snake-like creatures, while the Kraken typically has a more cephalopod-like appearance with tentacles.

7. The Sea Dragon:

The Sea Dragon, from Chinese mythology, is a powerful and benevolent creature that rules over the oceans. Unlike the Kraken, which is often associated with destruction and danger, the Sea Dragon is revered as a deity that brings blessings, rainfall, and protection to fishermen and sailors.

8. The Bunyip:

The Bunyip, from Australian Aboriginal mythology, is a mythical creature said to inhabit swamps and water bodies. It shares some similarities with the Kraken in terms of its association with water and mysterious nature. However, the Bunyip's appearance varies in different Aboriginal beliefs, whereas the Kraken has a more consistent and recognizable image.

In summary, while these sea monsters share some common themes of danger and association with water, they each have unique characteristics and narratives that make them distinct from the Kraken. The Kraken stands out as a colossal and terrifying sea monster from Norse mythology, while the other sea monsters encompass a wide range of appearances, motivations, and roles in their respective mythologies and cultural contexts.

Humanity's fascination with sea monsters is deeply rooted in psychological and sociological aspects that have shaped our beliefs, fears, and cultural narratives. The allure of sea monsters can be attributed to various psychological factors, including our curiosity about the unknown, our primal fears, and our desire to explore the mysteries of the deep sea. Additionally, the sociological aspects involve the influence of cultural storytelling, maritime traditions, and the ways in which sea monsters have been used to convey moral lessons and social norms.

Psychological Aspects:

1. Fear of the Unknown: The vastness of the ocean and the mysteries it holds have instilled a sense of wonder and fear in humans throughout history. Sea monsters represent the enigmatic and unexplored aspects of the deep sea, tapping into our fear of the unknown and the potential dangers lurking beneath the surface.

2. Coping Mechanism: Myths and legends, including sea monsters, often serve as a way for communities to cope with the uncertainties and dangers of their environment. By

personifying these fears as monstrous creatures, humans may feel a sense of control over the uncontrollable forces of nature.

3. Curiosity and Imagination: Our innate curiosity drives us to explore and explain the world around us. Sea monsters spark our imaginations, allowing us to envision fantastical creatures and scenarios that go beyond the constraints of reality.

4. Symbolic Meanings: Sea monsters can symbolize primal fears, chaos, and the untamed forces of nature. They embody the struggle between humans and the wild, reflecting our desire to conquer and understand the natural world.

Sociological Aspects:

1. Cultural Storytelling: Sea monsters have been a part of cultural storytelling across different societies for centuries. These myths and legends are passed down through generations, contributing to the collective identity and heritage of communities.

2. Maritime Traditions: The ocean has played a vital role in human history, serving as a means of exploration, trade, and travel. Maritime cultures often develop their unique stories about sea monsters as a way to pass down knowledge about the perils of the sea and to instill respect for its power.

3. Moral Lessons: Sea monster stories have often been used as cautionary tales, conveying moral lessons about the consequences of disobedience, arrogance, or greed. These narratives serve to reinforce social norms and codes of conduct, especially for sailors who faced real dangers at sea.

4. Entertainment and Artistic Expression: Sea monsters have become a popular subject in literature, art, and media. From classic myths to modern movies and video games, sea monsters continue to captivate audiences and inspire creative works.

Humanity's fascination with sea monsters is a multifaceted phenomenon, blending psychological intrigue with sociological influences. These mythical creatures tap into our curiosity about the unknown and represent our fears and awe of the ocean's depths. Throughout history, sea monsters have been woven into the fabric of human culture, providing moral lessons, reflecting our relationship with the natural world, and inspiring artistic expressions. The enduring appeal of sea monsters showcases the timeless and universal aspects of human imagination and storytelling.

THE KRAKEN QUEST: EXPLORING THE MYTHICAL GIANTS OF THE SEA

Chapter 9: The Kraken in Maritime Folklore

The Kraken has played a significant role in sailors' superstitions and beliefs throughout maritime history. As a legendary sea monster, the Kraken became a symbol of the dangers and mysteries of the deep sea, leading to various maritime superstitions and rituals. The Kraken's presence in sailors' beliefs was a reflection of their fears, uncertainties, and the need to make sense of the perils they faced at sea.

1. Fear of the Unknown: The ocean has always been a vast and mysterious realm, with dangers lurking beneath the surface. The Kraken, as an enormous and mythical sea creature, epitomized the unknown and the potential dangers faced by sailors. Belief in the Kraken served as a way for sailors to explain unexplained phenomena, such as treacherous waters or sudden storms, by attributing them to the presence of the mythical creature.

2. Navigational Caution: Sailors in the past relied on celestial navigation and rudimentary maps to navigate the seas. The fear of encountering the Kraken led sailors to avoid uncharted or dangerous waters, contributing to the development of maritime traditions and navigation practices.

3. Sacrificial Offerings: In some seafaring cultures, sailors believed in appeasing sea monsters like the Kraken with offerings or rituals. These offerings might include sacrifices or

prayers to ensure safe voyages and protect against the creature's wrath.

4. Warnings and Moral Lessons: The Kraken became a cautionary tale for sailors, reminding them of the perils of the sea and the consequences of arrogance or disobedience. Stories of ships and crews falling victim to the Kraken served as warnings, encouraging sailors to exercise caution and respect the power of the ocean.

5. Cultural Traditions: Belief in the Kraken became ingrained in maritime cultures, influencing folklore, stories, and traditions passed down through generations of sailors. These stories fostered a sense of camaraderie among sailors and reinforced the idea of facing adversity and dangers together as a crew.

6. Influence on Nautical Literature and Art: The Kraken's presence in sailors' superstitions has been a recurring theme in nautical literature, art, and songs. It has been depicted in sea shanties and depicted in maritime paintings, further perpetuating its mythical status in maritime culture.

7. Psychological Comfort: Belief in sea monsters like the Kraken provided psychological comfort for sailors facing the uncertainties and dangers of long sea voyages. The belief in supernatural forces might have served as a coping mechanism, offering a sense of control or explanation in the face of the unpredictable sea.

In modern times, as knowledge of the natural world and science has expanded, the belief in sea monsters like the Kraken has waned significantly. However, the Kraken's legacy continues to influence maritime folklore and popular culture, remaining an iconic figure in the collective imagination and memory of sailors' superstitions and beliefs.

Maritime rituals and practices aimed at appeasing or warding off the Kraken, like other sea monsters, were prevalent in the past when sailors relied on superstitions and folklore to navigate the treacherous waters. These rituals were performed to seek protection and ensure safe voyages while at sea.

1. Sacrificial Offerings: In some maritime cultures, sailors believed in offering sacrifices to sea monsters like the Kraken. These offerings could include animals, food, or even valuables thrown overboard as a symbolic gesture to appease the creature and seek its favor for a safe journey. By sacrificing something of value, sailors hoped to gain protection against the perceived wrath of the Kraken.

2. Prayers and Invocations: Sailors would often perform prayers and invocations to seek protection from sea monsters, including the Kraken. These rituals were meant to appeal to higher powers or benevolent sea deities for safe passage through the dangerous waters. Sailors believed that by invoking divine protection, they could ward off the Kraken's potential threat.

3. Protective Talismans and Symbols: Sailors would carry or place protective talismans and symbols onboard their ships to safeguard against sea monsters. These could include amulets, charms, or symbols believed to possess protective powers. For

example, images of sea deities or talismans representing the power of the ocean might be used to ward off the Kraken's malevolent influence.

4. Avoiding Uncharted Waters: To minimize the risk of encountering sea monsters like the Kraken, sailors would often avoid uncharted or dangerous waters. This avoidance was a practical approach to reducing potential encounters with mythical creatures and hazards that were associated with specific regions.

5. Rituals for Safe Departure and Arrival: Sailors would perform rituals before departure and upon arrival at their destinations to seek protection and express gratitude. These rituals might include prayers, offerings, or symbolic gestures to appease the Kraken and other sea entities during the voyage.

6. Offering Seafood to Sea Monsters: In some cultures, it was believed that offering seafood to sea monsters would appease them and ensure safe passage for the ship and its crew. Seafood, being associated with the ocean, was thought to have a special significance in pacifying sea creatures.

It is essential to recognize that these maritime rituals and practices were deeply rooted in the superstitions and beliefs of the time, and their efficacy was more psychological than scientific. Over time, as navigation and maritime practices evolved, reliance on such rituals diminished. Today, with advances in science and navigational technology, sailors no longer adhere to these traditional practices to ward off sea monsters like the Kraken. However, the legacy of these customs can still be seen in maritime folklore and cultural traditions that continue to enrich the maritime heritage of different seafaring communities.

The impact of Kraken stories on the morale and mental state of seafarers was profound and multifaceted. These mythical tales had both positive and negative effects on the psychological well-being of sailors throughout history. While Kraken stories could instill fear and anxiety, they also played a role in fostering camaraderie, offering a sense of control, and providing a coping mechanism for the challenges faced at sea.

Positive Impact:

1. Sense of Camaraderie: Kraken stories were often shared among sailors, creating a sense of camaraderie and shared experience. The belief in sea monsters like the Kraken became a unifying factor among the crew, bringing them together as they faced the perils of the unknown and unpredictable seas.

2. Coping Mechanism: Belief in the Kraken and other sea monsters served as a coping mechanism for the uncertainties and dangers of long sea voyages. By attributing adverse events or natural phenomena to the presence of sea creatures, sailors could gain a sense of control over the uncontrollable forces of nature.

3. Motivation for Caution: The fear of encountering the Kraken encouraged sailors to exercise caution and vigilance while at sea. This motivation for caution could lead to safer navigation practices and a heightened awareness of potential dangers, reducing the risk of accidents.

4. Connection to Maritime Traditions: Kraken stories were part of maritime traditions and cultural heritage, providing a link to the past and a sense of identity for seafaring communities. These stories helped preserve the wisdom and experiences of past generations of sailors.

Negative Impact:

1. Heightened Anxiety: The belief in sea monsters, including the Kraken, could lead to heightened anxiety and fear among sailors. The constant dread of encountering such creatures could negatively impact their mental state, making them more susceptible to stress and apprehension.

2. Deterioration of Morale: The fear of the Kraken and other sea monsters could deteriorate sailors' morale during long and challenging voyages. The persistent worry about encountering mythical creatures might lead to a sense of hopelessness and despair, affecting their overall well-being and motivation.

3. Superstitions and Fatalism: Belief in sea monsters could reinforce superstitious thinking and fatalism among sailors. They might attribute adverse events solely to supernatural forces, disregarding other practical factors, and undermining their confidence in their abilities as skilled seafarers.

4. Impact on Decision-Making: The fear of the Kraken might influence sailors' decision-making processes, causing them to make choices based on irrational fears rather than sound navigational judgment. This could potentially lead to suboptimal decisions that affect the safety of the crew and the success of the voyage.

THE KRAKEN QUEST: EXPLORING THE MYTHICAL GIANTS OF THE SEA

Kraken stories had a significant impact on the morale and mental state of seafarers, both positively and negatively. While these tales fostered a sense of camaraderie, provided coping mechanisms, and encouraged caution at sea, they also elicited anxiety, affected morale, and sometimes led to superstitious thinking. As navigation and maritime practices evolved, and as scientific knowledge expanded, the belief in sea monsters like the Kraken gradually waned, reducing their influence on seafarers' mental states. Nonetheless, the legacy of Kraken stories continues to be a part of maritime folklore and cultural heritage, reflecting the enduring fascination with the enigmatic depths of the ocean and the challenges faced by those who venture upon it.

EDWARD TURNER

Chapter 10: Kraken Sightings and Modern Reports

Currently there has been no confirmed or scientifically verified sightings of the Kraken or any other giant sea monster. The Kraken remains a mythical creature with its origins firmly rooted in Norse mythology and maritime folklore. However, it's essential to note that there have been occasional reports of large and unusual marine animals or phenomena that some individuals may interpret as potential Kraken sightings. Here are some examples of alleged Kraken sightings and related phenomena in recent times:

1. "Newfoundland Blob" (2001):

In 2001, a large, gelatinous mass washed ashore in Newfoundland, Canada. The mysterious creature was described as a 30-feet-long mass with tentacles, leading to speculations and media coverage suggesting it might be a Kraken. Subsequent analysis by marine biologists identified it as the remains of a basking shark carcass, which had decomposed and lost most of its features, leading to the bizarre appearance.

2. "St. Augustine Monster" (1896):

In 1896, a massive carcass washed ashore near St. Augustine, Florida. The creature was estimated to be around 21 feet long and was initially reported as a possible sea serpent or Kraken.

The carcass eventually decomposed beyond recognition before any definitive identification could be made, leading to debates and speculations about its true nature.

3. Large Squid Sightings:

Giant and colossal squids are real animals that dwell in the deep sea, and sightings of these creatures may have contributed to Kraken legends. While these species have been known to science for some time, they were rarely observed in their natural habitat until relatively recently. In recent times, advances in deep-sea exploration technology have led to more frequent encounters with giant squids, revealing their elusive nature and size.

It's important to approach alleged Kraken sightings with a critical and scientific mindset. Many of these sightings turn out to be misidentifications, decomposed remains of known marine animals, or sensationalized stories that feed into the Kraken mythology. As our understanding of the ocean and its inhabitants continues to evolve, we are better equipped to distinguish between real marine creatures and mythical sea monsters.

While the Kraken remains a captivating figure in human imagination and continues to inspire storytelling and artistic expressions, its existence as a real-life creature remains firmly in the realm of mythology and folklore.

From a scientific perspective, the alleged Kraken sightings and related reports must be evaluated critically and rigorously. When examining such claims, scientists rely on empirical evidence, established research methodologies, and expert analysis to determine their credibility. Here's an evaluation of the mentioned reports:

1. "Newfoundland Blob" (2001):

The initial media coverage and speculation about the "Newfoundland Blob" being a Kraken were based on limited information and visual observations. However, marine biologists and experts later examined the remains and identified them as a decomposed basking shark carcass. The identification was based on scientific knowledge of known marine species and their decomposition processes. The evidence provided by marine experts and the lack of any conclusive evidence supporting the Kraken hypothesis contribute to discrediting this alleged sighting.

2. "St. Augustine Monster" (1896):

The "St. Augustine Monster" case is from the late 19th century, and the lack of advanced scientific tools and methodologies at the time makes it challenging to assess the credibility of the sighting objectively. The creature's remains decomposed beyond recognition, preventing any definitive identification. Without concrete evidence or biological samples for modern analysis, it is impossible to draw scientific conclusions about the creature's identity. As a result, this report remains unverifiable and inconclusive from a scientific standpoint.

3. Large Squid Sightings:

Sightings of giant and colossal squids have been reported by sailors and researchers over the years. While these sightings are now better understood due to advances in deep-sea exploration technology, some earlier reports might have contributed to Kraken legends. However, the scientific community now recognizes giant and colossal squids as real, albeit elusive, creatures with known biological characteristics. The existence of these squids is supported by the recovery of physical specimens and photographic evidence. Therefore, the sightings of these squids are credible, verified by scientific research and physical evidence.

Overall, when evaluating reports of alleged Kraken sightings from a scientific perspective, it is crucial to distinguish between real, scientifically validated observations and those based on speculation, misidentification, or lack of concrete evidence. Scientific credibility relies on empirical evidence, rigorous examination, and an understanding of known biological species and natural processes. While some sightings may remain unexplained or open to interpretation, others can be confidently attributed to real marine creatures, such as giant and colossal squids. As the scientific understanding of the ocean continues to advance, any future reports of marine phenomena will be subject to more robust investigation and analysis.

Eyewitness accounts and misidentification have both played significant roles in Kraken sightings and reports of other mysterious sea creatures. Understanding the contributions of these factors is crucial in evaluating the credibility and validity of such sightings.

THE KRAKEN QUEST: EXPLORING THE MYTHICAL GIANTS OF THE SEA

Eyewitness Accounts:

1. Subjectivity and Perception: Eyewitness accounts are subjective and influenced by individual perceptions, biases, and beliefs. People may interpret and describe what they see differently based on their prior knowledge, cultural background, and personal experiences. In the case of Kraken sightings, eyewitnesses may be predisposed to associate unusual marine phenomena with mythical sea monsters due to cultural influences and folklore.

2. Memory and Accuracy: Human memory is fallible and can be affected by various factors such as time elapsed since the sighting, emotional intensity, and cognitive biases. As time passes, memories may become distorted or embellished, leading to inaccuracies in the recollection of the event. This can contribute to inconsistencies or discrepancies in Kraken sighting reports.

3. Emotional Impact: The fear or awe experienced during a sighting can influence the way eyewitnesses remember and describe the event. Emotions can affect attention and focus, potentially leading to the exaggeration of details or the misinterpretation of natural phenomena as something more extraordinary, like a Kraken.

4. Social Influence: Eyewitnesses may be influenced by the accounts of others, especially if they are part of a close-knit maritime community where tales of sea monsters are prevalent. Social pressure or a desire to fit within the accepted narrative

can impact how eyewitnesses interpret and report their sightings.

Role of Misidentification:

1. Unfamiliarity with Marine Life: At sea, sailors encounter various marine animals, some of which may be unfamiliar or rarely seen. Misidentification can occur when sailors encounter a species they are not familiar with, leading to confusion about its identity. Unusual behaviors or appearances may further contribute to the belief that the sighting was a Kraken.

2. Decomposed or Distorted Remains: In some cases, marine animals that wash ashore or are caught in fishing nets may be in an advanced state of decomposition. Decomposed remains can lose recognizable features, leading to speculative interpretations and confusion about the creature's identity.

3. Optical Illusions: The marine environment can present optical illusions, especially in conditions like fog or rough seas. These illusions may lead to misperceptions or misinterpretations of the size, shape, and behavior of marine animals.

4. Limited Visibility: Sighting conditions at sea can be challenging, especially during stormy weather or low light conditions. Poor visibility can hinder accurate identification, leading to ambiguous or mistaken reports.

Eyewitness accounts and misidentification both have substantial impacts on Kraken sightings and reports of other mysterious sea creatures. While eyewitness testimony is essential for collecting data and understanding phenomena, it is essential to recognize its limitations, subjectivity, and potential biases. Misidentification, influenced by unfamiliarity with marine life and challenging sighting conditions, can lead to reports that are later attributed to the mythical Kraken. As scientific knowledge and technology continue to advance, researchers can better distinguish between genuine observations of real marine creatures and those influenced by perception, misidentification, and cultural influences.

96

Chapter 11: Environmental Impact and Conservation

As a mythical creature, the Kraken does not exist in today's oceans. However, for the purpose of exploration, we can consider the ecological impact of a hypothetical Kraken-like creature—a massive, tentacled, and apex predator inhabiting the deep sea. Such a creature would have significant implications for marine ecosystems and the balance of oceanic food webs.

1. Top Predator and Trophic Cascade: As an apex predator, the Kraken-like creature would occupy the top position in the food chain. Its presence would exert top-down control on the populations of its prey, leading to a trophic cascade—where changes at the top level impact lower trophic levels. This could result in changes in abundance and distribution of prey species, potentially leading to indirect effects throughout the ecosystem.

2. Prey Species Distribution: The presence of a Kraken-like predator could lead to shifts in the distribution and behavior of its prey species. Prey species might avoid areas where the predator is active, potentially altering their feeding patterns, breeding grounds, and migration routes.

3. Biodiversity and Species Competition: The introduction of a large, novel predator could trigger competition among existing predators in the ecosystem. Depending on the Kraken-like

creature's feeding habits and prey preferences, it could compete with other large marine predators, potentially leading to shifts in species composition and biodiversity.

4. Trophic Niche and Prey Regulation: The hypothetical Kraken-like creature would occupy a specific trophic niche in the ecosystem. Its feeding behavior could regulate the abundance of prey populations, impacting the distribution of other species and influencing ecosystem dynamics.

5. Nutrient Cycling: As an apex predator, the Kraken-like creature would consume large quantities of prey, releasing nutrients through excretion and decomposition. This could influence nutrient cycling in the deep sea, potentially affecting primary production and other nutrient-dependent processes.

6. Species Interactions: The presence of a Kraken-like predator would likely trigger various species interactions. For example, scavenger species might benefit from feeding on remains left behind by the creature, influencing their population dynamics.

7. Behavioral Responses: Other marine species might develop behavioral responses to avoid predation by the Kraken-like creature. This could impact their foraging patterns, reproduction, and overall behavior.

It is important to reiterate that the Kraken is a mythical creature, and any ecological impact described here is purely hypothetical. Real-world marine ecosystems are shaped by existing, scientifically documented species and ecological interactions. The introduction of a fictional creature would likely have unpredictable and far-reaching consequences, disrupting the delicate balance that has evolved over millions of years in the oceans. The hypothetical scenarios presented here serve as a thought experiment but should not be interpreted as representing real ecological dynamics in today's oceans.

Marine conservation efforts are of paramount importance to protect ocean ecosystems and ensure the sustainability of the planet's most vital life-supporting system. The oceans play a crucial role in maintaining global biodiversity, regulating the climate, supporting fisheries, and providing essential resources for human well-being.

1. Biodiversity Preservation: The oceans are home to a vast array of marine species, many of which have not even been discovered or studied. Marine conservation helps protect these diverse ecosystems and the unique species that call them home. Preserving biodiversity is crucial for ecosystem resilience and the balance of the natural world.

2. Climate Regulation: Oceans absorb a significant amount of carbon dioxide, a greenhouse gas responsible for global warming. Marine conservation efforts help maintain the health of marine ecosystems, allowing them to continue their role in climate regulation and mitigating the impacts of climate change.

3. Food Security: Over three billion people rely on seafood as their primary source of protein, making marine resources vital for global food security. Sustainable fisheries management and marine conservation practices ensure that fish populations are

not overexploited, maintaining a steady supply of seafood for current and future generations.

4. Economic Value: Healthy oceans support numerous economic activities such as fishing, tourism, transportation, and renewable energy production. Marine conservation efforts protect these economic sectors from depletion and degradation, ensuring long-term benefits for coastal communities and the global economy.

5. Ecosystem Services: Oceans provide essential ecosystem services, including nutrient cycling, waste disposal, coastal protection, and the provision of medicines derived from marine organisms. Protecting marine ecosystems ensures these services continue to benefit society and the environment.

6. Climate Change Adaptation: Coastal habitats such as mangroves, seagrasses, and coral reefs act as natural buffers against storms and coastal erosion. Marine conservation efforts help maintain and restore these vital habitats, enhancing climate change adaptation and resilience for coastal communities.

7. Cultural and Recreational Value: Oceans hold immense cultural significance for many communities worldwide. They also provide recreational opportunities for millions of people through activities like swimming, surfing, snorkeling, and scuba diving. Marine conservation ensures these values are preserved for future generations.

8. Global Collaboration: Oceans are transboundary entities, making their conservation a global responsibility. International

collaboration and cooperation among nations are essential to address global marine conservation challenges, such as overfishing, marine pollution, and habitat destruction.

9. Sustainable Development: Marine conservation efforts align with the principles of sustainable development, promoting the responsible use of marine resources while safeguarding the environment and future generations' needs.

10. Conservation of Endangered Species: Many marine species, including marine mammals, sea turtles, and sharks, are at risk of extinction due to human activities. Marine conservation initiatives aim to protect and recover these endangered species and their habitats.

By prioritizing marine conservation efforts, we can safeguard the health and resilience of the world's oceans, promoting a sustainable future for both humanity and the countless species that rely on these vital ecosystems. Taking action now to protect our oceans ensures their continued contributions to the well-being of the planet and all its inhabitants.

The intersection between cryptozoology and environmental advocacy lies in the potential impact of these mythical or unverified creatures on environmental conservation efforts. Cryptozoology is the study of unknown or hidden animals, often including creatures of folklore and myth, like the Kraken, Bigfoot, Loch Ness Monster, and more. While these creatures have not been scientifically proven to exist, they hold cultural significance and capture the human imagination. Environmental advocacy, on the other hand, involves efforts to protect and conserve the natural world and its biodiversity. The connection between these two fields can be explored in the following ways:

1. Conservation of Habitats: Many cryptids are purported to inhabit remote or pristine habitats, often areas of high ecological importance. Advocates of cryptozoology might argue that exploring these regions in search of elusive creatures could raise awareness about the value of these habitats and the need to protect them from environmental threats like deforestation or habitat destruction.

2. Ecotourism and Cultural Value: In regions where cryptids are believed to dwell, local communities may capitalize on cryptozoological beliefs to promote ecotourism. Visitors interested in cryptids might be drawn to these areas, providing economic incentives for conservation efforts. Additionally, cryptozoological creatures often hold cultural significance for indigenous communities, emphasizing the importance of preserving their cultural heritage and traditional knowledge.

3. Taxonomic Exploration: Some cryptozoological enthusiasts argue that the pursuit of unknown animals can lead to the discovery of new species. While the likelihood of finding mythical creatures is minimal, the exploration of unknown regions may indeed reveal previously unknown species. Discovering new species can highlight the importance of preserving biodiversity and ecosystems.

4. Public Engagement and Education: Cryptozoological creatures are popular in popular culture, movies, and literature.

Environmental advocates might use this interest to engage the public in discussions about conservation, biodiversity, and the importance of protecting natural habitats.

5. Separating Fact from Fiction: Engaging in cryptozoological investigations can be an opportunity to foster scientific curiosity and critical thinking. By examining reported sightings and exploring the evidence behind cryptids, individuals can develop a better understanding of the scientific method and how to differentiate between credible evidence and folklore.

However, it is essential to approach the intersection between cryptozoology and environmental advocacy with caution. While the interest in cryptids can draw attention to environmental issues, it is crucial to emphasize the importance of basing conservation efforts on evidence-backed research and established scientific methods. Cryptozoological investigations, by nature, lack the scientific rigor required for ecological studies and wildlife conservation.

In summary, the intersection between cryptozoology and environmental advocacy offers opportunities for public engagement, cultural preservation, and habitat conservation. However, it is essential to balance the fascination with mythical creatures with a commitment to evidence-based conservation efforts, ensuring the protection of real biodiversity and the ecosystems that support it.

EDWARD TURNER

Chapter 12: Kraken in Popular Culture and Merchandising

The Kraken's mythical and captivating nature has made it a popular figure in advertising, branding, and commercial products. Companies and marketers have leveraged the Kraken's iconic image to create a unique and memorable brand identity, often associating it with products and services that evoke mystery, power, or a sense of adventure. Here are some ways the Kraken has been utilized in the realm of advertising and branding:

1. Alcoholic Beverages: The Kraken has been prominently featured in the branding of several alcoholic beverage companies, especially rum brands. The creature's association with the sea and its mythical nature align well with the adventurous and mysterious themes often linked to rum consumption.

2. Sports Teams: Some sports teams have adopted the Kraken as their mascot or incorporated the creature into their branding. The Kraken's image conveys strength, power, and determination, making it an attractive symbol for athletic organizations.

3. Entertainment Industry: The Kraken has been a recurring theme in the entertainment industry, particularly in movies and video games. Its menacing presence is often used to create

thrilling and suspenseful scenarios, attracting audiences seeking captivating storytelling and special effects.

4. Gaming and Gambling: The Kraken's mystical and awe-inspiring image has been utilized in various gaming and gambling products, from online slots to tabletop games. Its presence adds a touch of fantasy and excitement to these experiences.

5. Clothing and Merchandise: The Kraken's imagery has been featured on clothing, accessories, and other merchandise. It appeals to consumers seeking unique and visually striking designs that stand out from conventional options.

6. Seafood and Food Products: Some seafood companies have used the Kraken's association with the sea to promote their products. This strategy plays on the mythical link between the creature and the ocean's bounty.

7. Theme Parks and Attractions: The Kraken has been used as a theme or attraction in amusement parks and water parks, where it adds an element of fantasy and intrigue to the visitor experience.

8. Advertising Campaigns: The Kraken has been featured in advertising campaigns for various products and services. Its mysterious and powerful image can be used to evoke emotions and draw attention to the brand.

It's essential to note that while the Kraken's image is often utilized for commercial purposes, it remains a fictional creature rooted in mythology and folklore. Companies and marketers leverage the Kraken's popularity and cultural resonance to connect with consumers seeking products or experiences associated with adventure, mystery, and the allure of the sea.

However, the commercial use of mythical creatures like the Kraken should be approached with sensitivity and respect for the cultural origins of these beings. Misappropriation or misrepresentation of cultural symbols can be problematic and may result in negative perceptions by certain communities. Marketers and advertisers must strike a balance between leveraging the Kraken's appeal and ensuring they do not perpetuate harmful stereotypes or cultural appropriation in their branding and advertising efforts.

The Kraken's image has had a significant impact on consumer culture and marketing, influencing consumer preferences, brand associations, and product appeal. Its mythical and awe-inspiring nature has made it a potent symbol that resonates with certain segments of the population, particularly those interested in adventure, fantasy, and the mysteries of the sea. Here are some key aspects of the Kraken's impact on consumer culture and marketing:

1. Brand Differentiation: Incorporating the Kraken's image into branding and marketing helps companies stand out from competitors by creating a distinct and memorable identity. The creature's unique visual characteristics and association with the sea make it an eye-catching and recognizable symbol.

2. Emotional Connection: The Kraken's mythical and powerful image evokes emotions such as awe, excitement, and

wonder. By associating their products with the Kraken, companies aim to create an emotional connection with consumers, fostering positive brand perceptions and loyalty.

3. Adventure and Fantasy Appeal: The Kraken's association with adventure and fantasy appeals to consumers seeking products and experiences that go beyond the ordinary. This appeal is particularly relevant in industries like alcoholic beverages, entertainment, and sports, where the allure of the extraordinary is highly valued.

4. Targeting Niche Audiences: The Kraken's image appeals to niche audiences with specific interests in mythology, folklore, and fantasy. By using the Kraken in marketing, companies can target these audiences more effectively, establishing a strong and loyal customer base.

5. Storytelling and Engagement: The Kraken's legend and mythical background provide a rich storytelling opportunity for marketers. Brands can create engaging narratives that weave the creature's mythology into their marketing campaigns, drawing consumers into captivating and immersive brand experiences.

6. Product and Packaging Design: Incorporating the Kraken's image into product design and packaging adds visual appeal and sets products apart on store shelves. It can also evoke a sense of excitement and adventure, making the product more enticing to potential buyers.

7. Trend and Pop Culture Influence: The Kraken's presence in popular culture, movies, and video games has contributed to its

influence on consumer culture. Brands leverage the creature's trendiness and cultural resonance to align their products with current pop culture interests.

8. Licensing and Merchandising: The Kraken's image has been licensed for various merchandise, further spreading its influence in consumer culture. Clothing, accessories, toys, and collectibles featuring the Kraken appeal to consumers who want to express their affinity for mythical creatures and fantasy themes.

However, it is essential for marketers to approach the use of the Kraken's image with sensitivity and respect for its cultural origins. Misappropriation or misrepresentation of cultural symbols can lead to backlash and negative perceptions from certain communities. Marketers should also ensure that the use of the Kraken aligns with their brand identity and values, as inauthentic or inappropriate associations can undermine the credibility of marketing efforts.

The Kraken's image has had a profound impact on consumer culture and marketing. Its mythical and mysterious nature captivates audiences, offering brands a powerful tool to create differentiation, emotional connections, and engaging storytelling. By leveraging the Kraken's appeal, companies can attract niche audiences, foster brand loyalty, and align their products with adventure, fantasy, and the allure of the unknown.

The appeal of Kraken-themed merchandise lies in its unique combination of mythical allure, adventure, and aesthetic appeal. The Kraken, as a legendary sea monster, carries cultural significance deeply rooted in maritime folklore and mythology, which resonates with individuals interested in fantasy and the mysteries of the sea.

1. Fantasy and Mythical Allure: The Kraken embodies the sense of wonder and fantasy that captivates individuals of all ages. Its portrayal as a giant, tentacled creature dwelling in the depths of the ocean sparks the imagination, making it a fascinating subject for merchandise, art, and storytelling.

2. Nautical and Adventure Themes: The Kraken's association with the sea and seafaring adventures adds a sense of nautical charm to merchandise. It appeals to those with an interest in maritime history, exploration, and the allure of distant horizons.

3. Aesthetic and Visual Appeal: The Kraken's distinctive appearance, with its tentacles and menacing presence, lends itself to visually striking designs that stand out in the marketplace. The creature's unique and captivating imagery attracts consumers seeking merchandise with a bold and memorable look.

4. Connection to Pop Culture: The Kraken's presence in movies, books, and video games has cemented its status as a pop culture icon. This exposure has further contributed to the appeal of Kraken-themed merchandise, as fans seek to connect with beloved characters or stories featuring the mythical creature.

5. Symbolism and Personal Meaning: For some individuals, the Kraken carries symbolic significance. It may represent strength, resilience, or the ability to overcome challenges, making it a meaningful choice for personal accessories or décor.

6. Cultural Heritage and Folklore: The Kraken's cultural significance lies in its presence in the folklore and mythology of various maritime communities. Utilizing Kraken-themed merchandise allows people to connect with these cultural roots, preserving and celebrating these traditions.

7. Lifestyle and Subcultures: Kraken-themed merchandise can also be associated with specific lifestyles or subcultures. For example, it might appeal to enthusiasts of fantasy literature, role-playing games, or alternative fashion styles that embrace dark or occult aesthetics.

8. Merchandising Opportunities: From clothing and accessories to home décor and collectibles, Kraken-themed merchandise presents diverse opportunities for creative design and product development. This wide range of options allows companies to cater to various consumer preferences and interests.

Cultural Significance:

The Kraken's cultural significance is deeply intertwined with maritime traditions, particularly in regions with a strong seafaring heritage. In such communities, the Kraken symbolizes the unpredictability and dangers of the sea, becoming a cautionary tale for sailors and a symbol of the unknown depths below. Its presence in maritime folklore adds a sense of shared identity and history for those connected to seafaring trades.

Beyond its nautical significance, the Kraken's image has transcended cultural borders and gained broader appeal due to its portrayal in popular culture and media. It represents a bridge between history and contemporary storytelling, attracting audiences with its evocative and enigmatic presence.

The appeal of Kraken-themed merchandise lies in its mythical allure, nautical charm, and visual aesthetics. Its cultural significance is deeply rooted in maritime folklore and mythology, connecting people with their heritage and offering a sense of wonder and adventure. As a symbol of fantasy and the mysteries of the sea, Kraken-themed merchandise appeals to a diverse audience, from pop culture enthusiasts to those seeking unique and visually captivating products.

113

Chapter 13: The Kraken in Religion and Mythology

The Kraken, as a mythical sea creature, does not have direct religious significance in ancient belief systems like established deities or sacred figures. However, the Kraken and similar legendary sea monsters have held symbolic importance in the mythologies and belief systems of various cultures around the world. These symbols often represent primal fears, the unknown depths of the ocean, and the chaotic forces of nature. Here are some examples of the symbolic significance of sea monsters, including the Kraken, in ancient belief systems:

1. Chaos and Primordial Forces: In many ancient mythologies, sea monsters symbolized chaos, disorder, and the primordial forces of the ocean. These creatures were associated with unpredictable and destructive aspects of nature, reflecting the awe and fear that people held towards the vast and mysterious seas.

2. Maritime Folklore and Superstitions: In seafaring cultures, the Kraken and other sea monsters were subjects of maritime folklore and superstitions. Sailors would recount tales of these mythical creatures to explain unexplained phenomena or natural disasters at sea, attributing them to the actions of powerful and capricious sea spirits.

3. Symbol of Danger and Warning: Sea monsters, including the Kraken, were often depicted on maps and navigational charts

as a warning to sailors of dangerous waters or uncharted territories. These depictions served as visual reminders of the perils of the sea and the need for caution during voyages.

4. Sacrifice and Propitiation: In some cultures, sea monsters were believed to be spirits or deities that demanded appeasement through rituals or sacrifices. By offering tribute to these creatures, ancient seafarers sought protection and favorable conditions for their voyages.

5. Moral Lessons and Metaphors: Sea monsters also served as metaphors in ancient myths, teaching moral lessons or representing internal struggles and temptations. They symbolized challenges and obstacles that heroes had to overcome in their journeys, representing the human struggle against the unknown and the forces of chaos.

6. Connection to Underworld and Afterlife: In certain belief systems, sea monsters were associated with the underworld or the realm of the dead. They were believed to be guardians of the deep, where the souls of the deceased might reside. In this context, encountering a sea monster could symbolize a journey between life and death.

7. Element of Wonder and Curiosity: Sea monsters fascinated ancient cultures, sparking curiosity and wonder about the mysteries of the ocean. They often became central figures in mythological stories that attempted to explain natural phenomena and the origins of the world.

It's important to recognize that the symbolic significance of sea monsters like the Kraken varied widely across different cultures and time periods. While some cultures feared these creatures as harbingers of doom and chaos, others may have revered them as powerful deities or guardians of the deep. The symbolism and religious significance of sea monsters were influenced by the beliefs, experiences, and cultural context of each civilization, making them rich and diverse symbols in ancient belief systems.

The Kraken, as a mythical sea creature, does not have a prominent role in creation myths or cosmological narratives of ancient civilizations. Creation myths typically focus on explaining the origins of the world, the universe, and the emergence of life, and they often involve deities or supernatural beings. The Kraken, being a relatively recent addition to mythology, does not feature in the creation myths of ancient cultures.

However, sea monsters and giant creatures do appear in some cosmological narratives, particularly in the context of primal chaos and the forces of nature. These narratives often portray the ocean as a place of primordial chaos and the origin of all existence. Here are a few examples of sea monsters and their roles in cosmological narratives:

1. Tiamat in Mesopotamian Mythology: In Mesopotamian mythology, Tiamat is a primordial goddess representing the saltwater ocean. She is depicted as a monstrous sea dragon, and in the Enuma Elish, the Babylonian creation myth, Tiamat plays a central role in the cosmological narrative. The myth describes a battle between Tiamat and the younger gods, with

Marduk eventually slaying her to create the world from her body.

2. Apep in Egyptian Mythology: In Egyptian mythology, Apep (also known as Apophis) is a giant serpent associated with chaos and darkness. He is often depicted as an enemy of the sun god Ra, attempting to prevent the sun from rising and bringing chaos to the world. Apep represents the chaotic forces that the gods must overcome to maintain order in the cosmos.

3. Leviathan in Hebrew and Christian Traditions: Leviathan is a sea monster mentioned in various religious texts, including the Hebrew Bible and Christian scriptures. It is often associated with chaos and the forces of evil. In some interpretations, Leviathan is considered a symbol of the primordial ocean and the untamed elements of nature.

While the Kraken itself does not have a direct role in creation myths or cosmological narratives, it is worth noting that the concept of sea monsters and their association with chaos and primal forces is present in various cultures. Sea monsters often represent the untamed power of the ocean, embodying the idea of the unknown and mysterious depths of the sea.

It's important to recognize that creation myths and cosmological narratives vary greatly across different cultures and time periods. Each civilization's mythology provides unique insights into its worldview and cultural beliefs about the origin and nature of the universe. The Kraken's role in modern mythology and popular culture reflects humanity's ongoing fascination with the mysteries of the ocean and the enduring appeal of mythical sea creatures.

While the Kraken itself does not appear in religious texts, there are parallels between this mythical sea creature and other similar monstrous beings found in various religious and mythological traditions. These creatures share common themes related to chaos, the forces of nature, and the untamed power of the sea. Here are some examples of mythical creatures with similarities to the Kraken:

1. Leviathan (Hebrew Bible and Christian Scriptures): Leviathan is a sea monster mentioned in several religious texts, including the Hebrew Bible (Job 41; Psalms 74:14, 104:26) and the Christian Old Testament. Like the Kraken, Leviathan is associated with the deep sea and represents chaos and the untamed forces of nature. In some interpretations, Leviathan is depicted as a monstrous sea serpent or dragon.

2. Tiamat (Mesopotamian Mythology): In Mesopotamian mythology, Tiamat is a primordial goddess representing the saltwater ocean. She is often depicted as a monstrous sea dragon or serpent. Like the Kraken, Tiamat embodies the chaotic forces of the sea and is a symbol of primordial chaos.

3. Jörmungandr (Norse Mythology): In Norse mythology, Jörmungandr is a giant sea serpent, one of the three monstrous children of the god Loki. Jörmungandr is so large that it encircles the world, holding its tail in its mouth. Like the Kraken, Jörmungandr represents the power and unpredictability of the ocean.

4. Apep (Egyptian Mythology): Apep, also known as Apophis, is a giant serpent associated with chaos and darkness in Egyptian mythology. Apep is an enemy of the sun god Ra, and it attempts to prevent the sun from rising, symbolizing the forces of chaos that threaten order in the world.

5. Cetus (Greek Mythology): In Greek mythology, Cetus is a sea monster sent by the god Poseidon to terrorize the city of Aethiopia. Like the Kraken, Cetus represents the menacing and destructive forces of the sea.

These mythical creatures share a common theme of representing the power and unpredictability of the ocean. They embody the fear and awe that ancient cultures felt toward the vast and mysterious depths of the sea. These sea monsters often symbolize chaos, the unknown, and the forces of nature that humans struggled to understand and control.

In addition to their symbolic significance, these mythical sea creatures played roles in religious narratives, cosmological beliefs, and cultural traditions. They were used to explain natural phenomena, reinforce moral lessons, and emphasize the eternal struggle between order and chaos.

While the Kraken itself may not be present in religious texts, its parallels to these other mythical sea creatures illustrate the universality of human fascination with and reverence for the power and mysteries of the ocean in various cultural and religious contexts.

THE KRAKEN QUEST: EXPLORING THE MYTHICAL GIANTS OF THE SEA

Chapter 14: Cryptozoology and the Kraken

Cryptozoology is a pseudoscientific field that deals with the study and investigation of creatures or beings that are reported to exist based on anecdotal evidence, folklore, or other unverified sources. The term "cryptozoology" comes from the Greek words "kryptos," meaning hidden or secret, and "zoology," the study of animals. Cryptozoologists often focus on creatures known as "cryptids," which are animals that are rumored to exist but have not been scientifically proven to do so.

Cryptozoology operates on the assumption that there may be undiscovered or unknown species that have not yet been recognized by mainstream science. Researchers in this field use various methods, including eyewitness testimonies, folklore, historical accounts, and alleged sightings, to collect information about cryptids. They may also investigate physical evidence, such as footprints, hair samples, or photographs, to support the existence of these creatures.

The approach to the Kraken in cryptozoology is similar to that of other cryptids. While the Kraken is a mythical sea monster with origins in Scandinavian folklore and literature, some cryptozoologists have speculated that it may be based on encounters with real, but unidentified, marine creatures. They propose that the Kraken might be a remnant of a long-extinct giant cephalopod or another undiscovered species living in the depths of the ocean.

Cryptozoologists aim to bring credibility to their field by employing scientific-sounding methodologies, such as using a systematic approach to investigate sightings, conducting field research, and analyzing physical evidence. However, critics argue that the lack of concrete evidence and reliance on anecdotal accounts make cryptozoology more akin to folklore and speculative fiction than to mainstream science.

It is important to note that the scientific community generally does not consider cryptozoology as a legitimate scientific discipline. The methodology and lack of empirical evidence in cryptozoology do not meet the rigorous standards of scientific investigation and peer review. Mainstream science relies on the scientific method, empirical evidence, and reproducible results to build knowledge about the natural world.

While cryptozoology captures the imagination and fascination of some enthusiasts and serves as a source of entertainment and storytelling, it is essential to distinguish it from mainstream biology and zoology. The Kraken, as a mythical sea creature, remains firmly within the realm of folklore, literature, and popular culture, rather than scientific reality.

Scientific criticism and skepticism surrounding cryptozoological research stem from several key issues that cast doubt on the validity and credibility of the field. These issues include:

THE KRAKEN QUEST: EXPLORING THE MYTHICAL GIANTS OF THE SEA

1. Lack of Empirical Evidence: One of the most significant criticisms of cryptozoology is the lack of concrete, empirical evidence supporting the existence of cryptids. Despite numerous alleged sightings and anecdotes, cryptozoologists have not provided verifiable physical evidence, such as remains, DNA samples, or unambiguous photographs, to substantiate their claims.

2. Reliance on Anecdotal Accounts: Cryptozoology heavily relies on eyewitness testimonies, folklore, and historical accounts as primary sources of evidence. However, anecdotal accounts are subjective and prone to error, misidentification, exaggeration, or fabrication. In contrast, mainstream scientific research prioritizes empirical data and rigorous methodologies to support claims.

3. Methodological Concerns: The methodologies employed by cryptozoologists often lack scientific rigor and are criticized for being subjective, biased, and unverifiable. There is a lack of standardized protocols for investigating cryptids, leading to inconsistency in data collection and analysis.

4. Cherry-Picking and Confirmation Bias: Critics argue that cryptozoologists may selectively choose evidence that supports their preconceived beliefs in the existence of cryptids while ignoring or dismissing evidence that contradicts these beliefs. This confirmation bias can skew interpretations and conclusions.

5. Lack of Peer Review and Publication: Cryptozoological research is rarely published in reputable scientific journals,

undergoes rigorous peer review, or is subjected to scientific scrutiny. The absence of peer-reviewed publications limits the field's ability to gain acceptance within the scientific community.

6. Lack of Reproducibility: Reproducibility is a cornerstone of scientific inquiry, allowing others to verify and build upon research findings. The lack of replicable evidence in cryptozoology undermines its scientific credibility.

7. Absence of Testable Hypotheses: Many cryptozoological claims are based on loosely defined descriptions or vague characteristics of cryptids, making them difficult to test or falsify. In contrast, scientific hypotheses should be clearly defined and testable.

8. Mixing Myth and Reality: Cryptozoology often investigates creatures rooted in folklore, mythology, and popular culture, such as the Kraken, Bigfoot, or Loch Ness Monster. While these creatures capture the imagination, they are firmly situated in the realm of mythology and not within the purview of scientific inquiry.

As a result of these criticisms, cryptozoology is generally regarded with skepticism by the mainstream scientific community. Many scientists view the field as pseudoscientific or as more closely aligned with folklore and speculative fiction than with empirical scientific research.

While the idea of unknown or undiscovered species can be intriguing, scientific skepticism emphasizes the need for evidence-based inquiry, critical thinking, and adherence to rigorous methodologies. Mainstream science invites open inquiry and exploration but requires adherence to scientific principles to build knowledge about the natural world.

Cryptozoological investigations, despite facing scientific criticism, have both potential benefits and drawbacks. It is important to consider these aspects when evaluating the significance and impact of research in this field:

Potential Benefits:

1. Biodiversity Discovery: Cryptozoological investigations may lead to the discovery of new or previously unknown species. While the likelihood of finding legendary creatures like the Kraken is minimal, exploration of remote or understudied areas could uncover new species that have eluded scientific discovery.

2. Conservation Awareness: Cryptozoology can raise awareness about the importance of conservation and protection of natural habitats. By engaging the public with mythical or mysterious creatures, researchers may foster interest in wildlife preservation and environmental issues.

3. Cultural and Folklore Preservation: Cryptozoological investigations often involve studying folklore and traditional stories associated with cryptids. This research can help preserve cultural heritage and provide insight into the beliefs and values of different communities.

4. Scientific Curiosity: Exploring cryptids can spark scientific curiosity and interest in fields like biology, zoology, and marine

ecology. Young people who are fascinated by the prospect of unknown creatures may be inspired to pursue careers in science.

5. Ecotourism and Economic Impact: In regions with cryptozoological legends, interest in cryptids can attract tourists and generate economic opportunities for local communities. This can provide incentives for preserving natural habitats and traditional knowledge.

Potential Drawbacks:

1. Misallocation of Resources: Cryptozoological investigations can divert time, funding, and attention away from more critical scientific research and conservation efforts focused on known species and environmental issues.

2. Scientific Credibility: The lack of empirical evidence and rigorous methodologies in cryptozoology can undermine the field's scientific credibility. This may lead to its dismissal by the mainstream scientific community and hinder collaborations with legitimate researchers.

3. Ethical Concerns: Some cryptozoological investigations may involve searching for cryptids in sensitive or protected habitats, potentially causing disturbance or harm to local wildlife and ecosystems.

4. False Hope and Disappointment: The pursuit of cryptids, particularly legendary creatures, may give false hope to believers and enthusiasts who hope for their discovery.

Continuous lack of evidence can lead to disappointment and disillusionment.

5. Cultural Sensitivity: The exploration of cryptids rooted in cultural folklore must be approached with sensitivity and respect for the communities involved. Misappropriation or misrepresentation of cultural symbols can lead to backlash and negative perceptions.

6. Pseudoscience and Misinformation: Cryptozoological claims, especially when presented without scientific evidence, can contribute to the spread of pseudoscience and misinformation, misleading the public about the scientific process and the natural world.

Cryptozoological investigations offer potential benefits such as the discovery of new species, raising awareness about conservation, and preserving cultural heritage. However, they also face drawbacks, including the misallocation of resources, lack of scientific credibility, ethical concerns, and the potential to perpetuate pseudoscience and misinformation. It is essential to strike a balance between the intrigue of exploring mythical creatures and maintaining scientific integrity, prioritizing evidence-based research and adherence to scientific principles.

EDWARD TURNER

Chapter 15: Kraken and Climate Change

As a mythical sea creature, the Kraken is not subject to real-world impacts like climate change. However, we can consider the hypothetical impact of climate change on deep-sea creatures in general, drawing insights from existing scientific knowledge of deep-sea ecosystems.

Climate change is already affecting the world's oceans, including the deep-sea regions. Here are some potential impacts of climate change on deep-sea creatures:

1. Temperature Changes: As global temperatures rise, the deep-sea environment may experience changes in water temperature. Deep-sea creatures are adapted to cold and stable conditions, and even small changes in temperature could disrupt their physiological processes, reproductive cycles, and overall survival.

2. Ocean Acidification: Increased carbon dioxide levels in the atmosphere lead to ocean acidification. This can have adverse effects on deep-sea organisms, especially those with calcium carbonate shells, as acidic conditions can hinder shell formation and weaken existing shells.

3. Changes in Ocean Currents: Climate change can alter ocean currents, potentially affecting nutrient availability and food distribution in the deep sea. Many deep-sea creatures rely on

a steady supply of organic matter that sinks from the surface waters. Changes in currents could disrupt this food source.

4. Habitat Loss: Climate change can cause the melting of polar ice and lead to sea-level rise, which could affect deep-sea ecosystems near the continental slopes. Deep-sea creatures that rely on specific seafloor habitats could face habitat loss and reduced access to essential resources.

5. Oxygen Depletion: Global warming can exacerbate oxygen depletion in the deep sea, leading to "ocean deoxygenation." Many deep-sea creatures have low metabolic rates and are sensitive to changes in oxygen levels. Oxygen-depleted areas could become unsuitable or uninhabitable for certain species.

6. Range Shifts: As environmental conditions change, deep-sea creatures may need to adjust their distribution and migrate to find suitable habitats. However, some species might not be able to migrate fast enough to keep up with the pace of climate change, leading to localized extinctions.

7. Increased Vulnerability to Other Stressors: Climate change can increase the vulnerability of deep-sea creatures to other stressors, such as pollution, overfishing, and habitat destruction. These cumulative effects could further impact the resilience and survival of deep-sea species.

It is essential to recognize that our understanding of deep-sea ecosystems is limited, and studying these environments presents significant challenges due to their remote and inaccessible nature. Therefore, the full extent of climate change impacts on deep-sea creatures remains an area of ongoing research and scientific inquiry.

Overall, climate change poses significant threats to marine ecosystems, including the deep sea. To protect and conserve deep-sea biodiversity, it is crucial to mitigate the causes of climate change and implement measures that promote sustainable management and conservation of these unique and fragile environments.

Shifts in oceanic environments due to factors like climate change and human activities could impact the potential discovery of cryptids in several ways:

1. Habitat Changes: Changes in oceanic environments can alter the distribution and availability of habitats. Some cryptids are believed to inhabit specific regions or niches in the ocean. If their preferred habitats are significantly altered or lost due to environmental shifts, the chances of discovering these cryptids in those areas may diminish.

2. Range Expansions or Contractions: Cryptids, if they exist, may have specific ranges in the ocean where they are more likely to be encountered. Environmental changes could lead to shifts in the distribution of cryptids, either expanding or contracting their range. This could increase the chances of encountering them in new areas or make them harder to find in their historical locations.

3. Displacement and Migration: Environmental changes can force marine species, including potential cryptids, to migrate to new areas in search of suitable conditions. This displacement

could increase the likelihood of encountering cryptids in regions where they were not previously observed.

4. Altered Ecological Interactions: Environmental shifts can impact the dynamics of marine ecosystems and alter the interactions between different species. Cryptids, if they exist, may have specific ecological roles and interactions with other marine life. Changes in these interactions could affect the behavior and distribution of cryptids, making them more or less visible to human observers.

5. Impact on Food Sources: Some cryptids are hypothesized to be top predators or large marine animals with specific dietary requirements. Changes in oceanic environments could affect the abundance and distribution of their prey species. If food sources become scarce or change their behavior, it could influence the behavior and visibility of potential cryptids.

6. Human Exploration and Technology: As technology and human exploration of the deep sea continue to advance, our ability to search and survey remote oceanic regions improves. New underwater vehicles, sensors, and sampling techniques enhance our ability to explore and document the deep sea. These technological advancements increase the potential for discovering new species, including cryptids.

7. Oceanic Noise and Disturbance: Human activities in the ocean, such as shipping, fishing, and resource extraction, generate noise and disturbances that could affect the behavior and distribution of marine life, including potential cryptids. Increased anthropogenic noise pollution might make it harder

to detect cryptids or may drive them away from areas of human activity.

8. Fragmented and Limited Data: The vastness and inaccessibility of the deep sea, coupled with the relatively limited data available, create challenges for researchers studying marine life. Cryptids are often associated with remote or deep-sea regions that are difficult to explore comprehensively. Fragmented data can hinder our ability to detect or validate the existence of cryptids.

It is important to note that the potential discovery of cryptids is speculative, as there is currently no empirical evidence supporting their existence. While environmental shifts could theoretically impact the search for cryptids, it is essential to approach these investigations with scientific rigor, critical thinking, and adherence to established methodologies to distinguish between speculation and evidence-based research.

Researching cryptids in the context of environmental crises raises several ethical considerations that need careful examination:

1. Resource Allocation: In the face of pressing environmental challenges, allocating limited resources to investigate cryptids could divert attention and funding away from more critical conservation efforts and scientific research aimed at addressing real and urgent ecological issues.

2. Misuse of Resources: If resources are allocated to cryptid research without robust scientific justification, it may be

viewed as a misuse of funding and expertise that could be better directed towards solving tangible environmental problems.

3. Distraction from Conservation: Focusing on cryptid investigations might divert public attention and resources away from important conservation initiatives. It is essential to prioritize actions that directly contribute to preserving and restoring ecosystems and biodiversity.

4. Impact on Local Communities: In areas where cryptids are rumored to exist, researchers' activities might inadvertently disturb local communities or disrupt their traditional practices and belief systems. It is crucial to engage with and respect the concerns of local stakeholders in any research efforts.

5. Disruption of Ecosystems: Conducting research expeditions to search for cryptids could inadvertently disturb delicate marine ecosystems and their inhabitants. Researchers must ensure that their activities do not cause harm to local wildlife or habitats.

6. Misinformation and Sensationalism: Researching cryptids without clear scientific justification could perpetuate misinformation, sensationalism, and pseudoscience. This might undermine public trust in legitimate scientific research and conservation efforts.

7. Conservation Priorities: Efforts to protect and conserve the environment should be guided by scientific evidence and the best available knowledge. If cryptid research is pursued without a sound scientific basis, it may detract from conservation efforts grounded in evidence-based practices.

8. Ethics of Discovery: The discovery of new species, including cryptids, raises ethical questions about how to handle and protect them. Researchers must consider the potential impacts of discovery on these new species and the ethical responsibilities that come with it.

9. Respect for Indigenous Knowledge: In areas where cryptids are part of indigenous knowledge and folklore, researchers must approach their work with respect for local cultures and traditional beliefs. The rights and perspectives of indigenous communities should be taken into account.

10. Public Perception: Researching cryptids might be viewed skeptically or critically by the scientific community and the public, potentially affecting the credibility of the researchers involved and their broader scientific contributions.

While the idea of discovering new species, including cryptids, can be alluring, ethical considerations must guide research decisions in the context of environmental crises. Prioritizing efforts that directly contribute to addressing environmental challenges and conserving biodiversity is essential. If research on cryptids is undertaken, it should be grounded in sound scientific principles, conducted with transparency, and carried out with sensitivity to local communities and ecological impacts. Responsible and ethical research practices ensure that our efforts contribute positively to our understanding of the natural world and its conservation.

Chapter 16: Debunking Kraken Myths and Misconceptions

The Kraken, as a mythical sea creature, has captured the imagination of people for centuries and has been the subject of numerous misconceptions and inaccuracies. Here are some common ones:

1. Existence as a Real Creature: One of the most significant misconceptions about the Kraken is the belief that it is a real, living creature. While the Kraken has a rich history in Scandinavian folklore and literature, there is no scientific evidence to support its existence as a physical animal in the natural world.

2. Gigantic Size: The Kraken is often depicted as an enormous sea monster capable of reaching gigantic proportions, with tentacles capable of enveloping entire ships. In reality, no creature of such size has been discovered or documented in the natural world.

3. Attacks on Ships: In many fictional accounts, the Kraken is portrayed as a malevolent creature that attacks and sinks ships. While legends of sea monsters attacking vessels are prevalent in maritime folklore, there is no evidence to suggest that such events were caused by a real-life Kraken.

4. Octopus-like Appearance: The Kraken is often depicted as having a squid or octopus-like appearance with numerous long,

flexible tentacles. However, different accounts describe its appearance in various ways, and there is no consistent description across different myths and stories.

5. Deep-Sea Dwelling: While the Kraken is often associated with the deep sea and mysterious depths of the ocean, the specific details of its habitat vary in different tales. Some legends place it in deep underwater trenches, while others describe it as dwelling near the water's surface.

6. Scientific Classification: Some misconceptions suggest that the Kraken belongs to a specific scientific classification, such as being a type of giant squid or octopus. In reality, the Kraken is a mythical creature, and it does not fit into any known taxonomic group within the realm of biology.

7. Historical Accounts: Some sources claim that historical accounts and records support the existence of the Kraken. However, many of these accounts are exaggerated or misinterpretations of real-life events, and they are often conflated with other sea monster stories.

8. Cultural Universality: While the Kraken is well-known in Scandinavian folklore, not all cultures have an equivalent sea monster in their myths. The Kraken is a product of specific cultural traditions and does not have a universal presence in global folklore.

9. Association with the Bermuda Triangle: Some modern accounts and stories connect the Kraken to the Bermuda Triangle and its supposed mysterious disappearances. These

connections are purely fictional and not supported by any scientific evidence.

The Kraken is a mythical sea creature that has been the subject of various misconceptions and inaccuracies throughout history. It is essential to differentiate between folklore and reality when discussing the Kraken and other mythical creatures, recognizing them as imaginative tales rather than concrete scientific discoveries.

Sensationalized media reports and viral internet stories related to the Kraken often take advantage of the mythical creature's popularity to attract attention, clicks, and shares. They often exaggerate or distort information, leading to misinformation and confusion among the public. Here are some common ways sensationalism is applied to Kraken-related content:

1. Clickbait Headlines: Sensationalized media reports often use clickbait headlines to entice readers. These headlines may make bold claims about the discovery of a real Kraken or present exaggerated statements about its abilities or existence.

Example: "Scientists Shocked by Discovery of Gigantic Kraken in the Ocean Depths!"

2. Unsubstantiated Claims: Viral internet stories may make sweeping claims about the Kraken's existence or encounters without providing credible sources or evidence to support these assertions.

Example: "Fishermen Capture Incredible Footage of Kraken Attacking Boat! Is It Real?"

3. Out-of-Context Images: Sensational content may use unrelated or manipulated images to create the illusion of a Kraken sighting or encounter.

Example: Sharing an image of a large octopus or squid and falsely claiming it to be a Kraken.

4. False Testimonials: Some viral stories may feature alleged eyewitness testimonies or personal accounts of encounters with the Kraken. However, these testimonials are often fabricated or taken out of context to add credibility to the story.

Example: "Diver Shares Terrifying Encounter with the Fabled Kraken - I Thought I Was Going to Die!"

5. Lack of Scientific Sources: Sensationalized reports tend to lack credible scientific sources or experts' opinions to back up their claims. Instead, they may rely on anecdotal evidence or quotes from dubious sources.

Example: "Oceanographer Confirms Existence of Kraken - World's Most Elusive Sea Creature Found!"

6. Exaggerated Images and Videos: Some viral content may feature heavily edited or CGI-enhanced images and videos to create dramatic visual portrayals of the Kraken.

Example: Sharing a digitally manipulated video of an enormous sea creature to create the illusion of a real Kraken sighting.

7. Appeals to Emotion: Sensational stories often use emotional language and appeals to fear, curiosity, or astonishment to capture the audience's attention.

Example: "Chilling New Video Reveals the Kraken's Unearthly Roar - You Won't Believe Your Ears!"

8. Lack of Critical Analysis: Sensationalized content may avoid critical analysis or skeptical scrutiny of the claims being made, thereby perpetuating misinformation.

Example: "The Truth Behind the Kraken - Experts Astounded by Its Existence!"

It is essential for readers to approach sensationalized media reports and viral internet stories with skepticism and critical thinking. The Kraken is a mythical creature, and any claims about its existence should be viewed in the context of folklore, literature, and popular culture rather than scientific reality. Relying on credible sources, scientific evidence, and expert opinions is crucial to distinguish between factual information and sensationalized fiction.

Many phenomena that have been attributed to the Kraken in folklore and popular culture can be explained by natural events, known marine creatures, and other scientific phenomena. Here are evidence-based explanations for some common phenomena associated with the Kraken:

1. Shipwrecks and Mysterious Disappearances: Tales of ships being pulled underwater or mysteriously disappearing could be attributed to natural events such as powerful storms,

underwater currents, and rough seas. Additionally, navigational errors, human error, or maritime accidents could lead to shipwrecks without the involvement of a mythical creature.

2. Giant Squids and Other Large Cephalopods: Encounters with giant squids (Architeuthis dux) and other large cephalopods may have contributed to stories of the Kraken. These deep-sea creatures can reach considerable sizes and possess long, flexible tentacles, which could have been mistaken for the mythical sea monster.

3. Ocean Swells and Whirlpools: Reports of massive waves, whirlpools, and water disturbances in the ocean might be due to powerful ocean swells, tidal currents, or undersea geological phenomena rather than the actions of a mythical creature.

4. Seismic Activity: The Kraken's myth might have been influenced by seismic events such as underwater earthquakes or volcanic eruptions, which can cause sudden, violent disturbances in the ocean.

5. Giant Oarfish Sightings: Giant oarfish (Regalecus glesne) are rare deep-sea fish with long, serpent-like bodies. Their occasional sightings near the water's surface might have contributed to legends of sea serpents or monstrous creatures.

6. Whales and Other Marine Creatures: Encounters with large marine animals, such as whales, sharks, or sea turtles, could have been exaggerated or misinterpreted in the retelling, leading to the creation of mythical sea monster stories.

7. Underwater Volcanoes: The presence of underwater volcanic activity can create pockets of bubbles, foam, and discolored water, which may have contributed to stories of mysterious phenomena in the ocean.

8. Optical Illusions and Atmospheric Phenomena: Optical illusions, such as mirages or unusual atmospheric conditions, could distort the appearance of distant objects at sea, contributing to reports of strange and otherworldly sightings.

9. Myth and Folklore: The Kraken's legend likely originated from a blend of cultural beliefs, myths, and storytelling traditions. Stories of sea monsters and giant creatures have been a part of maritime folklore for centuries, passed down through generations.

While these evidence-based explanations provide plausible reasons for phenomena attributed to the Kraken, it is important to remember that folklore and mythology often blend fact and fiction. The Kraken's enduring popularity in culture is a testament to the enduring fascination with the mysteries of the deep sea and the allure of mythical creatures in the human imagination.

Chapter 17: Kraken in Modern Folklore and Urban Legends

The transformation of the Kraken myth in contemporary urban legends reflects the adaptability and evolution of folklore in the modern world. Urban legends are often shaped by popular culture, mass media, and the internet, and they tend to spread rapidly through word of mouth and social media. The Kraken, as a legendary sea monster, has been reimagined and incorporated into various urban legends with new twists and interpretations. Here are some ways in which the Kraken myth has transformed in contemporary urban legends:

1. Encounters in Modern Settings: In contemporary urban legends, the Kraken is often depicted as appearing in modern-day locations, such as lakes, rivers, or even urban environments. These new settings make the legend feel more relatable and relevant to people's everyday lives.

2. Connection to Mysterious Disappearances: Some urban legends link the Kraken to mysterious disappearances or unexplained events. These stories may involve people vanishing near bodies of water, with the Kraken as the alleged culprit.

3. Haunting Social Media and Viral Videos: With the rise of social media and the internet, urban legends about the Kraken may take the form of viral videos, hoaxes, or fictional accounts shared online. These stories can quickly gain traction and appear more believable due to the power of online sharing.

4. Creature of Revenge and Justice: In some contemporary urban legends, the Kraken is depicted as a vengeful creature seeking retribution for human actions that have harmed the environment or marine life. This portrayal reflects modern concerns about environmental degradation and the consequences of human actions on the planet.

5. Cross-Cultural Adaptations: As urban legends travel across cultures, the Kraken myth may blend with local folklore, resulting in new hybrid tales that incorporate elements from different traditions.

6. Cryptozoological Speculation: In the realm of cryptozoology and pseudoscience, the Kraken is sometimes discussed as a potential real-life creature that has eluded scientific discovery. These speculations add a layer of intrigue and mystery to the urban legend.

7. Artistic and Creative Expressions: Contemporary urban legends about the Kraken often find expression in various forms of art, including digital art, short films, and fictional stories. These creative works further propagate the legend and contribute to its transformation.

8. Pranks and Stunts: Some urban legends surrounding the Kraken might inspire pranks or staged events meant to deceive or entertain the public, blurring the lines between reality and fiction.

It's important to note that urban legends are not based on empirical evidence and should be viewed as part of storytelling traditions and popular culture rather than factual accounts.

THE KRAKEN QUEST: EXPLORING THE MYTHICAL GIANTS OF THE SEA

The transformation of the Kraken myth in contemporary urban legends reflects the enduring allure of sea monster stories and the adaptability of folklore in the modern age.

Internet culture has had a significant impact on the spread and evolution of Kraken-related folklore. The interconnectedness and speed of communication on the internet have facilitated the dissemination of stories, images, and memes, amplifying the influence of the Kraken myth in modern digital spaces. Here are some ways internet culture has influenced the spread of Kraken-related folklore:

1. Social Media Sharing: Social media platforms like Facebook, Twitter, Instagram, and Reddit provide a massive audience for sharing Kraken-related content. Memes, videos, and images related to the Kraken can quickly go viral, reaching a global audience within minutes.

2. User-Generated Content: The participatory nature of the internet allows users to create their own Kraken stories, artwork, and fan fiction, contributing to the growth and diversity of the Kraken mythos. Online communities dedicated to cryptids and sea monsters foster creativity and collaboration among enthusiasts.

3. Influencers and Creators: Internet influencers, content creators, and YouTubers often explore mysterious and fantastical topics, including mythical creatures like the Kraken. Their engagement with the myth amplifies its reach and popularity among their followers.

4. Online Forums and Discussion Boards: Websites like forums and Reddit host discussions about cryptids and mythical creatures, where users can share their own Kraken-related experiences or encounters, further propagating the folklore.

5. Digital Storytelling: The internet offers various storytelling formats, such as webcomics, podcasts, and interactive fiction, which enable creators to present Kraken-related tales in engaging and immersive ways.

6. Hoaxes and Pranks: The internet has also seen its share of Kraken-related hoaxes and pranks, where staged videos or fictional accounts are presented as real, testing the boundaries between fact and fiction.

7. Remix Culture: The remix culture of the internet allows users to reinterpret and reimagine the Kraken myth in various media, combining traditional folklore with contemporary elements and pop culture references.

8. Online Merchandise and Branding: Kraken-related merchandise, such as t-shirts, mugs, and posters, capitalize on the myth's popularity in internet culture. Online platforms like Etsy and Redbubble enable artists to sell their Kraken-themed creations worldwide.

9. Crowdsourcing Research: Online platforms have facilitated crowdsourced research and investigations into cryptids, including the Kraken. While not scientific in nature, these efforts contribute to the ongoing development of the Kraken legend.

10. Viral Challenges and Events: Internet challenges and events, such as "Kraken Week" or "Kraken Appreciation Day," can create temporary trends that promote the myth in playful and lighthearted ways.

As the Kraken myth is shared, remixed, and reinvented in internet culture, it becomes an ever-evolving entity that reflects the collective imagination and creativity of the online community. While internet culture has contributed to the widespread fascination with the Kraken, it is crucial to recognize that much of the content is fictional and falls within the realm of storytelling and popular culture, rather than scientific fact.

Technology and social media have had a profound impact on shaping the perception and propagation of cryptid tales, including creatures like the Kraken. These digital tools have revolutionized how folklore and myths are disseminated, discussed, and interpreted. Here are some ways technology and social media influence cryptid tales:

1. Global Reach: Social media platforms enable cryptid tales to reach a global audience quickly. Stories, images, and videos can be shared across continents in a matter of seconds, allowing folklore to transcend geographic boundaries and cultural barriers.

2. Viral Sensations: Cryptid tales, especially those presented in engaging formats such as videos or interactive content, have the potential to go viral on social media. This viral spread increases

their visibility and perpetuates their influence on popular culture.

3. User-Generated Content: Social media platforms encourage user-generated content, empowering individuals to share their personal encounters, sightings, or interpretations of cryptids. This participatory aspect of social media enriches the diversity of cryptid folklore and opens avenues for collective storytelling.

4. Online Communities: Online forums, groups, and subreddits dedicated to cryptids foster communities where enthusiasts can discuss, analyze, and share their thoughts about these creatures. Such communities fuel the growth of cryptid tales and create a sense of camaraderie among believers and skeptics alike.

5. Crowdsourced Research: Technology facilitates crowdsourced research efforts, where individuals collaborate to investigate cryptid tales, analyze purported evidence, and share findings. Online platforms provide spaces for sharing anecdotes, photographs, and audio recordings related to cryptids.

6. Digital Storytelling: Technology enables immersive storytelling experiences through podcasts, webcomics, interactive fiction, and augmented reality (AR) apps. These digital storytelling formats engage audiences and provide new ways to experience cryptid tales.

7. Image Manipulation and CGI: Advancements in image manipulation and computer-generated imagery (CGI) make it

easier to create convincing visual representations of cryptids. This can blur the line between fiction and reality, leading to more convincing and shareable content.

8. Debunking and Fact-Checking: While social media can perpetuate cryptid tales, it also serves as a platform for fact-checking and debunking. Skeptics and researchers can use these platforms to provide evidence-based explanations and challenge misinformation.

9. Branding and Merchandising: Cryptid tales, including the Kraken, lend themselves to branding and merchandising opportunities. Online stores offer a wide array of cryptid-themed merchandise, further solidifying their place in popular culture.

10. Citizen Journalism: With the rise of smartphones and social media, ordinary individuals can become citizen journalists, capturing and sharing alleged cryptid encounters or sightings in real-time. This real-time documentation adds to the perception of the tale's authenticity.

In summary, technology and social media have transformed the way cryptid tales, including the Kraken, are perceived, shared, and propagated. While these digital tools provide exciting opportunities for storytelling, community engagement, and artistic expression, they also present challenges in distinguishing between fact and fiction. It is essential for audiences to approach cryptid tales with critical thinking and awareness of their origins as folklore and popular culture rather than verified scientific phenomena.

Chapter 18: The Kraken and Science Fiction

The portrayal of the Kraken in science fiction literature and films often takes the mythical sea creature and reimagines it in futuristic or extraterrestrial settings. In this genre, the Kraken is frequently depicted as a monstrous and formidable creature that poses a threat to humanity, space travelers, or futuristic societies. Here are some common themes and elements found in the portrayal of the Kraken in science fiction:

1. Extraterrestrial Kraken: In science fiction, the Kraken is often portrayed as an alien creature from distant planets or unknown regions of space. It becomes an enigmatic and fearsome being with advanced technology and intelligence.

2. Space Exploration: Science fiction often places the Kraken in the context of space exploration and interstellar travel. Space-faring civilizations encounter the Kraken during their journeys through uncharted territories of the cosmos.

3. Genetic Engineering and Mutation: Some science fiction stories explore the idea of genetic engineering or mutation, resulting in the creation of genetically enhanced or mutated Kraken-like creatures that possess incredible abilities and adaptability.

4. Apocalypse and Post-Apocalyptic Worlds: The Kraken is sometimes associated with dystopian or post-apocalyptic worlds, where it emerges as a formidable force that contributes to the collapse of societies or wreaks havoc on the remains of civilization.

5. Symbol of Unknowable Nature: Science fiction often uses the Kraken as a symbol of the vastness and mystery of the universe. Its appearance reflects the idea that there are still countless unknown creatures and phenomena in the universe waiting to be discovered.

6. Battle with Futuristic Technology: In science fiction films and literature, the Kraken is often pitted against advanced technology and futuristic weapons. The clash between the ancient and the modern creates thrilling action sequences and dramatic tension.

7. Cosmic Horror: Some portrayals of the Kraken in science fiction draw on the theme of cosmic horror, emphasizing the creature's immense size, otherworldly appearance, and unfathomable intelligence. It becomes a source of existential fear and dread.

8. Environmental Themes: Science fiction stories featuring the Kraken may incorporate environmental themes, highlighting the impact of human activities on extraterrestrial ecosystems and the consequences of disturbing ancient or powerful entities.

9. Heroic Encounters: Protagonists in science fiction tales often face the Kraken as a daunting adversary. These encounters

test the characters' courage, ingenuity, and ability to overcome seemingly insurmountable odds.

10. Exploration of Human Nature: The Kraken's portrayal in science fiction allows for exploration of human nature and societal values. The creature becomes a mirror for human fears, desires, and aspirations, revealing deeper insights about humanity.

Overall, the portrayal of the Kraken in science fiction literature and films showcases the enduring allure of the mythical sea monster and its adaptability to imaginative storytelling. These portrayals continue to captivate audiences, offering thrilling tales of adventure, exploration, and the unknown in futuristic and otherworldly settings.

Speculative fiction, which includes genres such as science fiction, fantasy, and horror, plays a significant role in shaping public perceptions of cryptids, including legendary creatures like the Kraken. Speculative fiction allows authors, filmmakers, and artists to explore imaginative worlds, creatures, and scenarios that may exist beyond the boundaries of our current scientific understanding. Here are some ways in which speculative fiction influences public perceptions of cryptids:

1. Familiarization and Popularization: Speculative fiction introduces cryptids to a wider audience, familiarizing people with these mythical creatures and popularizing their stories. Cryptids that were once confined to regional folklore are now known worldwide due to their appearances in speculative fiction.

2. Visualization and Iconography: Speculative fiction provides visual representations and iconic imagery of cryptids, shaping how the public envisions these creatures. The visual portrayal of cryptids in books, movies, and artwork becomes a dominant reference for their appearance.

3. Emotional Connection: Through storytelling, speculative fiction creates emotional connections between the audience and cryptids. Readers and viewers become invested in the lives, struggles, and fates of these mythical creatures, leading to empathetic perceptions.

4. Exploration of Themes: Speculative fiction uses cryptids as metaphors to explore complex themes such as humanity's relationship with nature, fear of the unknown, ecological conservation, and the consequences of human actions on the environment.

5. Myth and Reality Blending: Speculative fiction blurs the lines between myth and reality, sometimes presenting cryptids as if they could exist in our world. This blurring can influence public debates on cryptid existence and generate discussions on the nature of truth and folklore.

6. Challenging Conventional Wisdom: Speculative fiction challenges conventional scientific explanations and invites readers to question the boundaries of what is possible. This can lead to broader discussions on the limits of human knowledge and the potential for new discoveries.

7. Creation of Cryptid Universes: Some speculative fiction works build complex cryptid universes with diverse species,

habitats, and histories. This world-building expands the public's understanding of cryptids beyond individual stories.

8. Cultivating Interest in Cryptozoology: Speculative fiction can inspire interest in cryptozoology, the study of hidden or unknown animals. Some readers/viewers may be inspired to explore the scientific basis of cryptids and engage with real-life investigations.

9. Cultural Exchange and Adaptation: Speculative fiction often brings together cryptids from different cultures and adapts them to new contexts. This exchange influences how cryptids are perceived and understood across cultures.

10. The Power of Imagination: Speculative fiction taps into the power of human imagination to create captivating and enduring tales. Public perceptions of cryptids are shaped by the imaginative storytelling that captures the collective fascination with the unknown and mysterious.

In summary, speculative fiction has a profound influence on shaping public perceptions of cryptids, serving as a bridge between myth and reality. By blending folklore, imagination, and scientific possibilities, speculative fiction contributes to the enduring appeal of cryptids in popular culture and keeps the mysteries of the natural world alive in our collective consciousness.

The intersections between science fiction and cryptozoological research are complex and multifaceted. Both fields explore the unknown and the speculative, but they approach their subjects from different perspectives. Here are some key intersections between science fiction and cryptozoological research:

1. Shared Interest in Unknown Creatures: Both science fiction and cryptozoological research are interested in creatures that are not yet confirmed or fully understood by mainstream science. Science fiction uses these unknown creatures as imaginative storytelling elements, while cryptozoological research seeks to investigate and document evidence of their existence.

2. Influence on Popular Culture: Both science fiction and cryptozoology have a significant impact on popular culture. Science fiction stories about cryptids have contributed to their enduring fascination and presence in movies, books, and other media. Cryptozoological research, when sensationalized or speculated upon, can also shape public perceptions and inspire new speculative fiction works.

3. Inspiration for Speculative Stories: Cryptozoological reports and legends about cryptids often serve as inspiration for science fiction writers and creators. These real-life mysteries provide rich source material for crafting imaginative tales of exploration, adventure, and encounters with unknown creatures.

4. Exploration of the Boundaries of Knowledge: Both fields involve exploration and inquiry into the boundaries of human knowledge. Science fiction pushes the boundaries of scientific understanding by imagining possibilities beyond our current understanding, while cryptozoological research seeks to

identify and document creatures that may challenge existing scientific classifications.

5. Use of Scientific Methods: Cryptozoological research strives to employ scientific methodologies to investigate cryptid reports. This includes conducting field research, collecting eyewitness accounts, analyzing evidence, and applying principles from fields like biology, zoology, and ecology. However, the scientific rigor of cryptozoology is often a subject of debate within the scientific community.

6. Tensions between Fiction and Science: Science fiction, by definition, is fictional and speculative. While some works may be grounded in scientific principles, many others involve fantastical elements. Cryptozoological research, on the other hand, seeks to bridge the gap between anecdotal evidence and scientific validation, leading to tensions between evidence-based practices and speculative claims.

7. Reflections of Cultural Beliefs: Cryptozoological reports and science fiction stories often reflect cultural beliefs, fears, and desires. Both fields can shed light on how societies interpret and interact with the unknown and the mysterious.

8. Potential for Mutual Inspiration: Cryptozoological reports and discoveries of new species in the natural world have, at times, provided inspiration for science fiction stories. Conversely, science fiction tales may lead to increased interest in cryptozoological research and prompt more investigations into potential cryptids.

The intersections between science fiction and cryptozoological research demonstrate the shared fascination with the unknown and the desire to explore the mysteries of the natural world. While science fiction offers imaginative and speculative tales, cryptozoological research seeks to validate and understand alleged cryptid sightings. These intersections highlight the dynamic relationship between storytelling, scientific inquiry, and the enduring allure of cryptids in human culture.

THE KRAKEN QUEST: EXPLORING THE MYTHICAL GIANTS OF THE SEA

Chapter 19: Legends Reimagined: Kraken in Modern Fantasy

In contemporary fantasy literature and media, the Kraken is often portrayed as a powerful and enigmatic creature that embodies the mystery and majesty of the sea. While its traditional depiction as a giant sea monster with massive tentacles persists, modern interpretations add depth and complexity to the Kraken's character. Here are some common themes and aspects of the Kraken's portrayal in contemporary fantasy:

1. Sentience and Intelligence: Contemporary fantasy often attributes sentience and intelligence to the Kraken, presenting it as a creature with thoughts, emotions, and motivations. This portrayal creates opportunities for the Kraken to be a more nuanced and multifaceted character.

2. Guardianship of the Oceans: The Kraken is frequently depicted as a guardian of the oceans, protecting marine life and the delicate balance of underwater ecosystems. It can serve as a symbol of environmental conservation and the importance of preserving the seas.

3. Mythical Wisdom: In some stories, the Kraken possesses mythical wisdom or ancient knowledge about the world and its secrets. Characters may seek out the Kraken for guidance or insights into their quests.

4. Redemption Arcs: Contemporary fantasy often explores redemption arcs for mythical creatures, including the Kraken. Some stories present the Kraken as a misunderstood or maligned being, giving it a chance for redemption and reconciliation with humans.

5. Connection to Humanity: Certain tales establish a connection between the Kraken and humanity, blurring the lines between monstrous and human attributes. Such connections can be explored through magical bonds, shared ancestry, or transformative curses.

6. Intricate World-Building: Contemporary fantasy allows for intricate world-building, presenting the Kraken as part of a larger mythological or magical ecosystem. It may coexist with other fantastical creatures and deities in richly imagined worlds.

7. Themes of Power and Responsibility: The Kraken's immense power often serves as a thematic element in contemporary fantasy, exploring questions of responsibility, restraint, and the consequences of wielding great power.

8. Emotional Depth: The Kraken's portrayal in modern fantasy can evoke a range of emotions, from fear and awe to empathy and compassion. Its character arc and interactions with other beings can evoke emotional responses from readers and viewers.

9. Fantasy Adventures: The Kraken frequently appears in epic fantasy adventures, playing a role in quests, battles, and journeys across fantastical realms and treacherous waters.

10. Humanizing Monsters: Contemporary fantasy challenges the notion of monstrousness by humanizing creatures like the Kraken. It explores themes of acceptance, tolerance, and the complex nature of good and evil.

Overall, the Kraken's depiction in contemporary fantasy literature and media goes beyond its traditional role as a fearsome sea monster. Through these modern interpretations, the Kraken becomes a symbol of the untamed, mysterious, and magical aspects of the natural world, capturing the imagination of audiences and reflecting the timeless fascination with legendary creatures.

Mythical creatures hold significant cultural importance in modern fantasy narratives, as they tap into timeless human beliefs, fears, and aspirations. They play multifaceted roles that reflect various aspects of human culture, psychology, and societal values. Here are some aspects of the cultural significance of mythical creatures in modern fantasy narratives:

1. Imagination and Escapism: Mythical creatures inspire imagination and provide a sense of escapism, transporting readers and viewers to fantastical worlds beyond the limits of reality. They offer a form of catharsis and freedom from the constraints of everyday life.

2. Symbolism and Allegory: Mythical creatures often symbolize abstract concepts, archetypes, and universal themes. They can represent primal fears, virtues, vices, and the complexity of human nature. As such, they become vehicles for conveying allegorical messages.

3. Exploration of Otherness: Through mythical creatures, modern fantasy narratives explore the theme of otherness, reflecting on human attitudes toward the unknown and the different. These creatures challenge readers to question prejudices and embrace diversity.

4. Moral Lessons and Ethical Dilemmas: The encounters with mythical creatures in fantasy narratives frequently lead to moral dilemmas and ethical choices for characters. These dilemmas offer opportunities for introspection and reflection on values and principles.

5. Reflection of Cultural Beliefs: The inclusion of mythical creatures often reflects cultural beliefs, folklore, and legends from various societies. They embody elements of cultural identity and heritage, adding depth and richness to the fantasy world.

6. Quest for Meaning and Purpose: Mythical creatures often play pivotal roles in characters' quests for meaning, purpose, and self-discovery. They act as catalysts for personal growth and transformation, driving the hero's journey.

7. Exploration of Nature and Environment: Many mythical creatures are closely tied to nature and the environment. Their portrayal in fantasy narratives allows authors to explore the interconnectivity between humans, the natural world, and the need for ecological balance.

8. Portrayal of Human Emotions: The characteristics and behaviors of mythical creatures can mirror human emotions, fears, and desires. Their interactions with characters provide

opportunities for emotional storytelling and character development.

9. Archetypal Heroes and Villains: Mythical creatures often serve as archetypal heroes or villains, embodying virtues or vices that resonate with the human psyche. They become symbolic representations of human virtues to aspire to or flaws to overcome.

10. Legacy and Tradition: The inclusion of mythical creatures in modern fantasy narratives honors the storytelling traditions of the past. It keeps cultural myths alive and encourages new generations to engage with the rich tapestry of folklore and legend.

In summary, mythical creatures in modern fantasy narratives serve as powerful storytelling devices that transcend cultural and historical boundaries. They ignite the imagination, symbolize human experiences, and provide opportunities for introspection and exploration of complex themes. Their enduring cultural significance lies in their ability to captivate and resonate with audiences, offering a bridge between the past and the present, the known and the unknown.

The influence of traditional folklore on the portrayal of the Kraken in modern fantasy is significant, as it provides the foundation for how this mythical sea creature is depicted and understood in contemporary storytelling. Traditional folklore shapes various aspects of the Kraken's character, appearance, and role in modern fantasy narratives. Here are some ways in which traditional folklore influences the portrayal of the Kraken in modern fantasy:

1. Origins of the Myth: Traditional folklore lays the groundwork for the Kraken myth, establishing its status as a legendary sea monster with roots in Scandinavian and Nordic mythology. Modern fantasy often retains the Kraken's foundational attributes, such as its immense size, tentacled form, and association with the deep ocean.

2. Nautical Folklore: Traditional nautical folklore and sailor tales contributed to the Kraken's image as a perilous and monstrous entity lurking in the depths of the sea. Modern fantasy continues to draw on these nautical elements, imbuing the Kraken with a sense of foreboding and danger.

3. Cultural Context: Traditional folklore is embedded in specific cultural contexts, and this context continues to influence how the Kraken is depicted in modern fantasy narratives. Depending on the story's setting and cultural background, the Kraken may take on different regional interpretations and characteristics.

4. Symbolism and Archetypes: Traditional folklore often attributes symbolic meanings to mythical creatures, and the Kraken is no exception. In modern fantasy, the Kraken can symbolize various themes such as chaos, the unknown, the destructive forces of nature, or the human struggle against overwhelming odds.

5. Heroic Encounters: Traditional folklore frequently features encounters between sailors and the Kraken, where heroes must

face and overcome the creature's menace. These heroic encounters continue to inspire modern fantasy narratives, driving protagonists' quests and journeys.

6. Cultural Continuity: Incorporating traditional folklore into modern fantasy ensures cultural continuity and preserves the historical roots of these myths. It allows contemporary audiences to connect with age-old stories and engage with the legacy of their cultural heritage.

7. Adaptation and Reinvention: While traditional folklore provides the basis for the Kraken's portrayal, modern fantasy also allows for creative adaptation and reinvention of the myth. Authors and creators can build upon the traditional narrative, adding new layers of complexity and depth to the Kraken's character.

8. Influence on Other Fantasy Creatures: The Kraken's portrayal in traditional folklore has influenced the depiction of other fantasy sea monsters and creatures. Elements of the Kraken's myth, such as its giant tentacles or deep-sea habitat, can be found in other creatures of fantasy literature and media.

9. Connection to Marine Conservation: In some modern fantasy narratives, the Kraken's portrayal is shaped by contemporary concerns about marine conservation and ecological balance. It serves as a reminder of the delicate relationship between humans and the oceans.

Traditional folklore forms the basis for the portrayal of the Kraken in modern fantasy, influencing its appearance, attributes, symbolism, and cultural context. By building on these foundational elements, modern fantasy continues to celebrate the enduring allure and fascination of this legendary sea monster while also allowing for fresh and imaginative interpretations.

Chapter 20: The Legacy of the Kraken: Reflections and Future Speculations

K ey Findings:

1. Historical Origins: The Kraken originated in Scandinavian and Nordic folklore as a giant sea monster with tentacles capable of pulling down entire ships.

2. Cultural Significance: The Kraken holds cultural significance across various civilizations, symbolizing the mysteries of the sea, the fear of the unknown, and the forces of nature.

3. Mythical Giants: The Kraken's portrayal as a colossal cephalopod has inspired myths and tales of other giant sea creatures in different cultures.

4. Modern Interpretations: In contemporary fantasy, science fiction, and cryptozoological research, the Kraken has been reimagined as an intelligent creature, guardian of the oceans, and a symbol of environmental conservation.

Enduring Mysteries:

1. Existence as a Cryptid: Despite numerous reports and legends, there is no scientific evidence confirming the existence of the Kraken or any other giant sea monster like it.

2. Misidentifications: Many alleged Kraken sightings can be attributed to misidentifications of known marine animals, such as squids, octopuses, or whales.

3. Historical Accuracy: The accuracy of historical accounts of the Kraken's encounters remains uncertain, with some tales potentially exaggerated or influenced by folklore.

4. Deep-Sea Exploration: The depths of the ocean remain largely unexplored, leaving room for the possibility of discovering new and undiscovered species, including giant cephalopods.

5. Environmental Impact: The potential impact of climate change and human activities on deep-sea ecosystems, and their inhabitants, including hypothetical Kraken-like creatures, remains a subject of ongoing research.

6. Scientific Credibility: The credibility of cryptozoological research into the Kraken and other cryptids is a subject of debate within the scientific community, as it often lacks rigorous scientific methodology.

In summary, the Kraken is a legendary sea creature with deep-rooted origins in folklore and mythology. Its portrayal in modern narratives and its influence on popular culture highlight its enduring fascination. However, the Kraken's existence remains unverified, leaving it among the enduring mysteries of the natural world and the human imagination. As scientific knowledge and exploration continue, some of the mysteries surrounding the Kraken may eventually be unraveled, while others may continue to captivate our imaginations for generations to come.

The enduring appeal and cultural significance of Kraken myths throughout history can be attributed to several factors that resonate with human psychology, storytelling traditions, and societal beliefs. These myths have captivated the human imagination for centuries and continue to hold a place in contemporary culture. Here are some key reasons for their enduring appeal and cultural significance:

1. Human Fascination with the Unknown: Kraken myths tap into the timeless human fascination with the unknown and the mysteries of the natural world. The vastness of the ocean, with its unexplored depths, has always been a source of wonder and fear, and the Kraken embodies these primal emotions.

2. Symbolism of Natural Forces: The Kraken represents the uncontrollable forces of nature, making it a symbol of the unpredictable and powerful aspects of the natural world. Its myth serves as a reminder of humanity's vulnerability and humility in the face of nature's might.

3. Marine Folklore and Nautical Traditions: The Kraken's cultural significance is deeply rooted in marine folklore and nautical traditions. For sailors and seafarers, the sea was both a source of livelihood and danger, and the Kraken myth provided a way to explain unexplained phenomena and instill caution among sailors.

4. Moral Lessons and Metaphors: Kraken myths often carry moral lessons and metaphors, addressing themes such as

bravery, hubris, and the consequences of human actions. They serve as cautionary tales and provide insights into human nature and the human condition.

5. Evolution of Narrative: The Kraken myth has evolved over time through storytelling, adapting to changing cultural contexts and new storytelling mediums. This adaptability has allowed the myth to remain relevant and appealing to each generation.

6. Influence on Art and Literature: The Kraken has inspired numerous works of art, literature, and media across history. Its depiction in paintings, literature, and films has contributed to its lasting cultural significance and widespread recognition.

7. Cross-Cultural Connections: The Kraken's myth transcends geographic and cultural boundaries, appearing in different forms in various civilizations. This universality contributes to its enduring appeal and its ability to connect people across different cultures.

8. Association with Sea Monsters: The allure of sea monsters and mythical creatures has been a part of human storytelling and folklore for millennia. The Kraken is part of a larger fascination with fantastical beings from the deep oceans.

9. Archetypal Hero's Journey: Kraken myths often involve heroes facing the creature in epic battles, following the archetypal hero's journey. These narratives resonate with audiences and provide a sense of adventure and triumph over adversity.

THE KRAKEN QUEST: EXPLORING THE MYTHICAL GIANTS OF THE SEA

10. Continuity in Modern Culture: The Kraken's presence in contemporary fantasy, science fiction, and popular culture ensures its continued relevance and cultural significance. It has become a timeless and iconic figure in the world of myths and legendary creatures.

The enduring appeal and cultural significance of Kraken myths can be attributed to their exploration of the human psyche, their symbolism of natural forces, their connection to marine folklore, and their adaptability across different cultures and storytelling traditions. As long as the ocean remains a vast realm of unexplored mysteries, the Kraken will continue to captivate the human imagination and inspire awe and wonder for generations to come.

The study of deep-sea creatures holds immense potential for exciting discoveries and developments in the future. As advancements in technology, exploration, and scientific research continue, we can anticipate several areas of progress in understanding and learning about these mysterious inhabitants of the ocean's depths:

1. New Species and Biodiversity: Deep-sea ecosystems are among the least explored areas on Earth. As scientists deploy more sophisticated sampling methods, such as remotely operated vehicles (ROVs) and autonomous underwater vehicles (AUVs), we can expect the discovery of numerous new species, expanding our understanding of deep-sea biodiversity.

2. Extremophile Adaptations: The deep sea presents a challenging environment with extreme pressure, cold

temperatures, and little to no sunlight. Studying deep-sea creatures will provide insights into their remarkable adaptations to survive and thrive in such harsh conditions.

3. Biotechnological Applications: Deep-sea organisms may hold valuable bioactive compounds and enzymes with potential biotechnological applications. Studying these creatures could lead to the development of new pharmaceuticals, enzymes, and materials.

4. Ecosystem Dynamics: Deep-sea ecosystems are intricately connected to global oceanic processes. Understanding these ecosystems and their interactions with the broader marine environment will contribute to a better understanding of the Earth's ecological balance.

5. Deep-Sea Food Webs: Exploring the trophic relationships among deep-sea creatures will shed light on the intricate food webs that sustain life in the abyss. This knowledge will have implications for fisheries management and conservation.

6. Behavioral Studies: Observing the behavior of deep-sea creatures in their natural habitats will provide insights into their social structures, mating behaviors, and communication methods, offering a more comprehensive understanding of their ecological roles.

7. Impact of Climate Change: As the effects of climate change reach the deep sea, scientists will investigate how these changes impact deep-sea ecosystems and species. Understanding these effects is crucial for marine conservation and environmental management.

8. Genetic Studies: Advances in genetic analysis techniques will enable researchers to study the genomes of deep-sea organisms, unraveling the genetic basis of their unique adaptations and evolution.

9. Marine Protected Areas: As the importance of deep-sea ecosystems becomes evident, efforts to establish marine protected areas (MPAs) in the deep ocean may increase, safeguarding vulnerable habitats and species.

10. Public Engagement and Education: The exploration and discovery of deep-sea creatures are fascinating to the general public. With improved communication and outreach efforts, the study of deep-sea creatures will engage and inspire people to care about ocean conservation.

The future of deep-sea creature research holds great promise for expanding our knowledge of these enigmatic beings and their critical role in marine ecosystems. As scientific technology and exploration continue to advance, we can expect groundbreaking discoveries that will contribute to marine conservation, biotechnology, and our understanding of the vast and mysterious world that lies beneath the ocean's surface.

Epilogue: In Search of the Unseen Depths

As we reach the end of our journey through "The Kraken Quest: Exploring the Mythical Giants of the Sea," it is evident that the allure of cryptids and the mysteries of the ocean are timeless and deeply ingrained in the human psyche. The Kraken, with its enthralling legend spanning centuries, epitomizes the enduring fascination with unknown creatures lurking in the depths of the sea. Throughout this book, we have delved into the historical origins, cultural significance, and modern interpretations of this mythical sea monster, finding its presence in ancient folklore as well as in contemporary fantasy, science fiction, and cryptozoological research.

The mysteries of the ocean, like the fathomless abyss itself, continue to beckon us with their irresistible allure. The vast expanses of unexplored waters remain a realm of enigma and wonder, where countless undiscovered creatures may still lurk. As our technology and understanding of the natural world advance, we find ourselves on the cusp of exciting discoveries that may bring to light new species, unveil ancient secrets, and illuminate the hidden intricacies of deep-sea ecosystems.

Yet, as we embark on this quest for knowledge, we must acknowledge that the allure of cryptids and the mysteries of the ocean go beyond empirical exploration. They resonate with something fundamental in the human spirit—the innate curiosity to explore the unknown, to dream beyond the horizon, and to seek answers to the most profound questions about our world and ourselves.

Cryptids like the Kraken serve as cultural touchstones, bridging the gap between imagination and reality, mythology and science. They challenge us to question the boundaries of what we know and to contemplate the wonders that may still lie hidden beneath the waves. In this process, we learn not only about the creatures of the deep but also about the intricacies of human culture, storytelling, and our relationship with the natural world.

The mysteries of the ocean are not confined to the realm of science and exploration; they extend to the depths of the human soul. They speak to our awe of nature's grandeur, our fear of the unknown, and our yearning for connection with the vastness of the cosmos. As we contemplate the mysteries of the deep, we are reminded of the humility that comes with acknowledging that there is much we have yet to learn, much we have yet to understand.

So, as we close the pages of "The Kraken Quest," let us carry with us the sense of wonder and reverence that this journey has evoked. Let us embrace the allure of cryptids and the mysteries of the ocean as a testament to the boundless curiosity of the human spirit. And, with every new discovery and revelation that comes our way, let us remain steadfast in our commitment to preserving the beauty and diversity of our natural world, so that future generations may continue to embark on their own quests for knowledge and understanding, forever captivated by the enduring allure of the unknown.

Sign up to my free newsletter to get updates on new releases, FREE teaser chapters to upcoming releases and FREE digital short stories.

Or visit https://tinyurl.com/olanc

I never spam and you can unsubscribe at any time.

Don't miss out!

Visit the website below and you can sign up to receive emails whenever Edward Turner publishes a new book. There's no charge and no obligation.

https://books2read.com/r/B-A-SYIZ-ASJMC

BOOKS 2 READ

Connecting independent readers to independent writers.

Also by Edward Turner

Ghosts of Paris: Ten Haunted Places in the City of Love
Appalachian Nightmares: The Top 10 Creepy Creatures of the Mountains
Asia's Top Ten Cryptids: Legends, Sightings, and Theories
Beyond the Shadows: Unlocking the Mystery of Bigfoot
Evil Women in History: Uncovering the Gruesome Crimes of Ten Notorious Female Killers
Ghosts of London: Ten Haunted Places in The City
Ghosts of New York: Ten Haunted Places in The Big Apple
Ghosts of Oregon: The Top 10 Haunted Places You Must Visit
Ghosts of the Stage: Ten Hauntings at the Theatre
Missouri Nightmares: The Top 10 Chilling Legends
Mothman Unleashed: Into the Darkened Skies
North America's Top Ten Cryptids: Legends, Sightings, and Theories
Philly's Phantom Encounters: Exploring the City's Most Haunted Places
Secrets of the Deep: The Mystery of the Loch Ness Monster
Unsolved Mysteries: Delving into the Shadows of Infamous Murders
Unveiling the Shadows: A Journey into Financial Crimes and Scandals

The Kraken Quest: Exploring the Mythical Giants of the Sea

About the Author

Edward Turner is a renowned author who specializes in exploring the realms of ghosts, the paranormal, and cryptids. With a captivating writing style and an insatiable curiosity for the unknown, Turner has garnered a dedicated following of readers who are captivated by his thrilling and eerie tales.

Born with an innate fascination for the supernatural, Turner has spent decades delving into the depths of paranormal phenomena, unearthing captivating stories and untangling mysteries that lie beyond the veil of the ordinary. His extensive research and meticulous attention to detail have earned him a reputation as a leading authority in the field.

Through his books, Turner expertly weaves together chilling accounts of encounters with ghosts, offering readers a glimpse into the ethereal world that coexists alongside our own. His ability to paint vivid portraits of spectral apparitions and convey the haunting atmosphere of haunted locations has made his works both spine-tingling and thought-provoking.

Turner's exploration of the paranormal doesn't stop at ghosts. He also dives into the fascinating world of cryptids—creatures that defy conventional explanation. His in-depth investigations into legendary creatures such as Bigfoot, the Loch Ness Monster, and the Chupacabra showcase his commitment to shedding light on these enigmatic beings.

With each page, Edward Turner's readers are drawn deeper into the enigmatic and unknown. His unique storytelling ability combined with his meticulous research has made him a sought-after author for those with an insatiable thirst for the supernatural. Whether delving into ghostly encounters or unraveling the mysteries of elusive cryptids, Turner's books offer a spine-chilling and immersive reading experience that leaves readers questioning the boundaries of our reality.

Edward Turner's works have earned critical acclaim and numerous accolades within the paranormal genre. He continues to explore the unexplained, captivating readers with his distinctive narrative style and unwavering dedication to unveiling the mysteries that lie hidden in the shadows.